AF265449

First published 2020
by Grum Goes Global

ISBN: 978-0-473-54647-2
Published in Hanmer Springs, Aotearoa New Zealand

www.facebook.com/Grum-Goes-Global
grumgoesglobal@gmail.com

This amazing adventure and book would not have been the same without the assistance, support, and encouragement of so many, too many to list. My thanks go out to you all.

Special thanks to:

My wonderful wife Juliet, for allowing me the 900 days, for inspiring me to ride to the next destination so I could meet her, for being available at all hours to listen to a tired, lonely husband, camped under a bush in far off lands, and providing support in so many ways. Love you always.

My children, Lisa and Paul, and their families.

Janie & all Juliet's work mates, friends and family for looking after her while I was away.

Verdon Kelliher.

The Cowie Family.

The Test of Time.

Kevin for building my bikes.

My friends who told me I was "frigging crazy", or "You can't do that" (you inspired me to prove you wrong).

All my hosts in 41 countries.

All those that joined me on the road on their bicycles, whether for just a few minutes, or for many long kilometers.

All those that read my blogs and sent me messages of support & encouragement.

All those that waved, shouted greetings, or joined me for selfies.

All those who have constantly nagged me to get my book written and Therese from KingFisher Publishing for leading me through the hurdles of producing a book.

And Fiona, you truly are a princess.

Thank also for the support of:

Hiking New Zealand - Bivouac Outdoors - First Training - Canteen NZ - Canteen Australia - Prostrate Cancer Awareness - Lions Clubs of Australia and New Zealand

Intro

This trip was always intended to be a journey, joining the dots. Cycling from places I have been before, to places I've never been. Revisiting special places, and finding new special places. Seeing for myself what others have talked about, places that previously I've only seen from 30,000 feet, places I've read about, or dreamed of visiting. The initial plan involved visiting 64 countries over four years and eight months. Ju said it was too long. Cut it in half.
So, there I was, on a 900 day, 50,000km, adventure, joining the dots in 41 countries.

Why?

I've flown several times around the world, and each time I've looked below and wondered: Who Lives there? What language do they speak? What is their life like, their religion, their money? What does their home look like?

At 61 years old I am almost the oldest male in my family ever. My uncle died at 54, my grandfather at 59, and my father at 65. There is still so much I want to see and do, and time could very possibly be getting short.

All my working life I have challenged others. Now I needed my own challenge. I don't like heights, so climbing Mt Everest was out. I get sea sick, so paddling or rowing across the Atlantic was out. Why not cycling a loop around the globe?

When I told my mates my plan, they told me I was "Feeking MAD", and there was no way I could do it.

How?

Juliet, my lovely wife, has been working for years to improve her education, after deciding that she wanted to get a Degree. She chose to become a Paramedic and worked extremely hard, over several years to achieve her dream job as an Intensive Care Paramedic on the Westpac Rescue Helicopter team.

While she was studying, we often missed out on adventures we might have together, so when she finally achieved her goal, and being such a wonderful caring wife, she suggested it was my time to follow my dream, to have my adventure. Yippee, I began planning. After some months of sorting through maps, planning routes, and guessing times, I approached her with my plan.

"I want to cycle around the world"

"Okay. How long will it take, and when will you leave"

"I'm going to cycle out of Melbourne on the 1st July 2014 and get back mid-August 2018. Just over four years."

"That's too long. Cut it in half."

Woohoo. I had 900 days of adventure coming my way.

We were already Warmshowers hosts, an international organisation that hosts Cycle Tourers, so we met lots of people to quiz about cycle touring. My mate, Kevin, had recently built me a Surly Karate Monkey Mountain bike. We had all sorts of outdoor gear. I just needed to get it in some sort of order. Winter of 2013 I took off for a lap around the North Island of New Zealand. I needed to know whether I had the correct gear, and more importantly, did I enjoy cycling for such a long time. I LOVED IT.

Refinement of the gear followed, and Kevin built me a new bike, with a few more places for bits and bobs to be attached. This time it was a Surly Ogre, a beautiful green machine, and her name popped into my head, just like a new-born child's name does, (Princess) Fiona. She was going to be my one companion for the duration of the adventure.

Books I had read about this type of adventure all had a cause, to deflect the "he's a nutter" comments. I decided on Prostrate Cancer Awareness, and Canteen (an organisation that supports teenagers coping with Cancer).

My son Paul and daughter Lisa gave me their blessing. We worked together to set up a Website and a Facebook page, and we gave the adventure a name: Grum Goes Global.

I had my route, I had my leave pass, I had my trusty steed, and I had my cause. I had an adventure waiting.

Joining the Dots

Book 4

Europe & USA

Grum Frith

EUROPE

GREECE, BULGARIA, SERBIA, KOSOVO, MACEDONIA, ALBANIA, MONTENEGRO, CROATIA, BOSNIA, SLOVENIA, ITALY, SAN MARINO, MONACO, FRANCE, ANDORRA, SPAIN, PORTUGAL

6921KM 131 DAYS

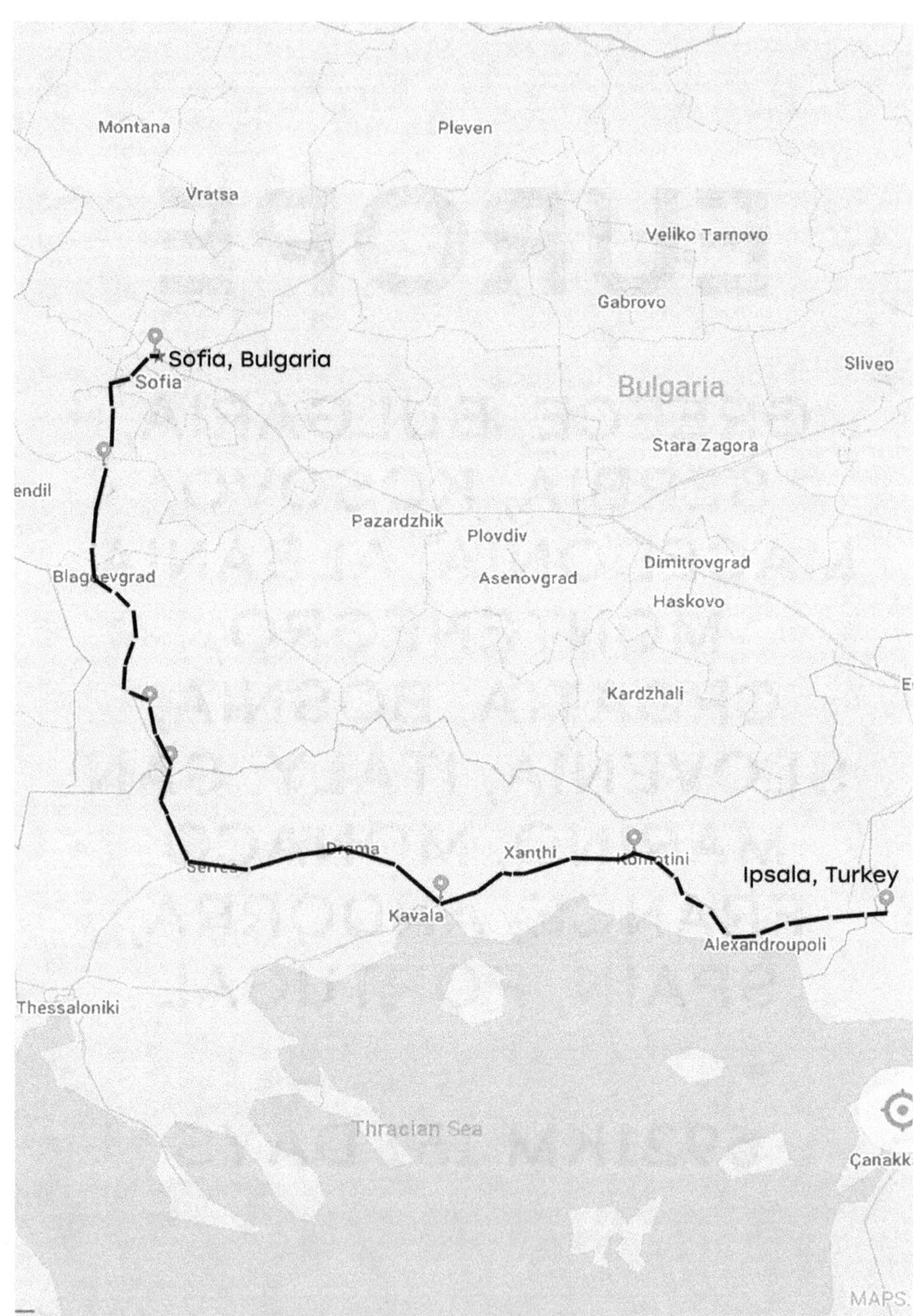

Montana
Pleven
Vratsa
Veliko Tarnovo
Gabrovo
Sofia, Bulgaria
Sofia
Bulgaria
Sliven
Stara Zagora
endil
Pazardzhik
Plovdiv
Blagoevgrad
Asenovgrad
Dimitrovgrad
Haskovo
Kardzhali
Drama
Xanthi
Komotini
Ipsala, Turkey
Serres
Kavala
Alexandroupoli
Thessaloniki
Thracian Sea
Çanakk
MAPS.

THE ADRIATIC

SUDDENLY SURROUNDED BY SANTAS

20th December 2015

Ipsala to Khomeini Greece 122km
To Nea Karvali Greece 96km

Crossing the border into my first European country couldn't have been easier. "Welcome to Europe. How long has it taken to get here? Have you been to Greece before? Let me give you your first European stamp. Have a Merry Christmas." And then I broke the law. For 40km I cycled on a motorway. I honestly didn't see the signs; they were hidden behind trucks, but the road was great, and empty.

I cycled into my first Greek city and it hits me that it's Christmas. Santa's are everywhere: carols, decorations, Christmas lights. Last year I was in Asia. No Santa's or Christmas there, so it's been a while. All I did was cross a border.

I found the legal road. It was glorious, smooth, quiet, passing through small villages, and no dog attacks. The hills were small, the straights short, and there were lots of bends. There were rivers, coastline and lakes to cycle besides, views of the Aegean Sea to the left, and mountains to the right. All I did was cross a border.

I stopped in a small village for supplies. "Where are you from?" "Wow a kiwi!" "Have you changed your flag yet?" "You shouldn't change it." All spoken in perfectly understandable English. Then from a group of ladies manning a "British School stall", selling cakes and Christmas toys: "You've cycled from NZ? Wow. Can we help you?" in English and all I did was cross a border.

Wow there's lots of good looking, athletic women riding bicycles. That's something I've missed. Haven't seen anything like that since I can't remember when. And all I did was cross a border.

Churches and priests singing.

Wow, there's lots of bird life about. A huge heron sanctuary, lots of hawks, sea birds, flocks of starlings. You don't realise what you're missing until it appears again.

I've got euros in my pocket, but they disappear quickly. Hotels are three times the price of Turkey, and ten times the price of those in South East Asia. Food is a lot more expensive as well, and all I did was cross a border.

GARLIC AND OLIVE OIL

22nd December 2015

Nea Karvali to Dimitra Greece 102km
To Sandanski, Bulgaria, 100km

This week, in 1977, my former wife Eileen, and I decided to cycle from Auckland to Whangarei, to spend Christmas with her family. Eileen whipped up some panniers on her sewing machine. I tied them to the bikes. We filled them with our tent, food and Christmas presents, and headed north, crossing to Devonport on the ferry. Our first ever cycle touring. I think we camped in Warkworth that night. It had been a tough ride. No training, no bike prep, just loads of luggage, and being the week before Christmas, busy roads. The head wind the next morning stretched us, and the Brynderwyn's were a challenge. Somewhere along the Waipu straights, I think Eileen's dad turned up in the car, and took all the luggage, and maybe even Eileen and her bike. We did not cycle back to Auckland.

Two years later, in April 1979, we were in Greece. It was 40°C, and we were on an island, on the beach, melting. I lasted less than a week, before I insisted, we go somewhere cooler, and where we could do something other than sweat, and dodge the sun. Who would have thought, that thirty-eight years later, I would be once again cycle touring, and in Greece? This time it's 4°C, while its 36°C at home, and I'm enjoying the cycling, and Greece, much more than those previous experiences.

Today I cycled 60 km along a stunning coastline, beautiful beaches, pretty towns and villages, castles, ancient walls, bridges, and towers. I was so tempted to go swimming in the clear blue waters, but 4°C made it just a little too challenging for this not so tough adventurer. I was very tempted to stop and camp at one of the bays, but yesterday was Sunday, and not much is open here on Sunday, so I had little food, not enough to last overnight. Then, just as I was about to leave the coast, I found my first supermarket, and a restaurant, but nowhere suitable to camp. I did however have a feast, chicken kebabs, baked potato, and toast. Everything was covered in garlic, and olive oil, just like I remember from 1979 and it was yummy. Another thing I remember from 1979 was the smell of very ripe cheese. No refrigeration in Greece way back then, and the cheese was kept under a damp cloth. Thankfully, the supermarket today was able to supply cheese that wasn't nearly as smelly.

10km after leaving the coast, just after summiting a rise, I find a cafe. The yummiest chocolate cake and hot chocolate I've had since leaving home. That, and the garlic and olive oil, have set me up for a night in the tent. I hope it doesn't get too cold.

On the road again, with a very frosted tent, and I'm heading towards the Bulgarian border. At one point a group of men are rearranging a detour, the road is very narrow, and I'm dodging trucks. The boss calls me over: "Hey Mr Kiwi. You can ride on our new motorway. It opens tomorrow, so no traffic, only you, so very safe." I don't have the heart to tell him I don't like motorways, but duck behind their vehicles, and for 30km cycle on a brand new, not yet open, motorway. And the wind is fierce, and cold, and in my face.

I pop out at the border. A Greek man stamps my passport. No one else wants to see it. I'm in the Republic of Bulgaria. Wow I'm back in an "Eastern bloc" country. I know because I visit a supermarket. It stocks sausage, tinned fish, biscuits, chocolate, pickles, vodka, cigarettes and condoms. What else do you need? There are a couple of hundred kilometers to the capital, Sofia, so I should make it by Christmas.

GETTING THE BALANCE

24th December 2015

Sandanski to Diakovo Bulgaria 106km
To Sofia Bulgaria 65km

It's 7am on Christmas Eve, and I'm in my tent on top of a hill. It's -10°C, and the tent fly is frozen solid. My sleeping bag is soggy from condensation, and my sweaty clothes from yesterday are still wet, but warm, from being inside my sleeping bag with me, but I'm busting for a pee! Damn.

It had been cold yesterday too, but I'd woken up in a hotel, with warm dry clothes. My first km though, had been up a slippery cobblestone street, and I was sweating by the time I got to the top. The next 2km was down a rutted farm track; brakes on full, and the sweat had frozen next to my skin. Hmmmm. Then the next 20km followed a very narrow road, busy with trucks, but the light was delicious, and I was following a beautiful tree lined river, so I warmed up, except for my left hand. Then I passed through a tunnel, and the next 60km was in freezing fog, with ice forming on my raincoat, gloves and glasses, and I'm sweating, because I'm working hard, even though my feet and hands are freezing. Hmmmm.

A second tunnel and I emerge onto a motorway. Hmmmm. Cycles are not usually allowed on motorways, but there is no option, and the road is wider, so safer for me, but I still can't see more than 50m. For 30km there is no exit, and only one service area, but it sells hot chocolate. Thaw time is delicious, but thawing frozen fingers is very painful, and the lady at the counter has never attended a customer relations course. Grumpy or what...

Finally, I find a motorway exit. I've done 100km and do not feel up to the 60km into Sofia. I break out above the freezing fog and I'm in an apple orchard, on top of a hill, bathed in sunshine: a camping spot. I even get to hang my soaked clothes on a tree for a couple of hours, in the sun. I've never before realised how much your body sweats when doing activity. In Nepal and India, it was obvious. I was drinking nine litres of water a day and not peeing. Here, I'm not drinking as much, but the sweat is still happening, but not evaporating in the heat; there is no heat. So, every item of very necessary clothing that keeps me warm on the flats, into the wind, and downhills, is soaked, lovely.

But today, Christmas Eve, nothing is dry. I'm okay packing up, but there is a chilling breeze, and I don't want to sit around, so decide I will eat along the road, hopefully in a warm cafe. As soon as I start riding, everything freezes, and when I drop down a hill into the freezing fog, snow like flakes form on my gloves, and raincoat. It looks rather Christmassy, my raincoat being red. After 30km I break out of the fog again. I'm very hungry. Never before in my life have, I been so connected to the types of food I've eaten. I'm always thinking, yep I've had protein, yep I've had fats, but I need more carbs, and vitamins. Right now, I need everything. I'm squeezed around a traffic island by trucks, who are jockeying for road space now they can see the road, and find a drain to rest in, to eat. I've got bread, cheese, biscuits, an apple, and a litre of frozen "slushy" orange juice, but the sun is shining on this spot, so once again the thaw starts. Eventually, my hands are warm enough to operate my phone, and look at my map. Bugger! I was meant to turn off at that roundabout 500m ago, damn it. I wheel the bike back, against the traffic, on a very busy motorway, and around the roundabout the wrong way.

5km downhill, and no fog, but there is another cafe, with another grumpy serving lady, but yummy warming hot chocolate, and Internet. No positive responses from any Warmshowers hosts, but a hostel recommendation, great. Then there is more downhill. The roads are busy, and icy, but it doesn't take long to reach the city. There are trams, and slippery tram lines, but I'm careful, and then slippery cobblestones again, but just over to the left, a cycleway, and it's not cobbled; woohooo.

Folk in the city seem pretty relaxed, and the cycleway takes me right to the door of the hostel, and a delightful hot shower, and they will put my clothes through a wash, which is great because all I have that is not soaked and frozen, is one pair of shorts and one shirt.

There are people here that speak English. A few Aussies, who I will tolerate because it's Christmas, a couple of Americans, some Poms, and some brash Canadians, but it means I can have real conversations. There's talk of going to Star Wars at midday tomorrow, Christmas Day, followed by a huge Christmas dinner. I turned down the midnight Mass invite. I reckon I'm getting the balance reasonably right. Only two exceptions: amount of Marmite carried, far too little; and length of time between Juju visits, far too long. Hope you had a merry one.

Niš
Vratsa
Leskovac
Sofia, Bulgaria
Vranje
Gjilan
Ferizaj
Kyustendil
Kumanovo
Blagoevgrad
Skopje, Macedonia
Veles
Shtip
North Macedonia
Prilep
Serres
Bitola

FOG, FUG N FUN

27th December 2015

Sofia to Perot, Serbia 86km

It was hard getting on the bike this morning. It was -2°C, and foggy. The assurance of one of the staff that the fog should only be around the city helped a little, as I left the warmth and comfort of the Hostel Mostel, and hit the soggy, bleak streets. I don't know how the locals live with it. It really is bleak.

30km later, I'm still in dense freezing fog, and I find the first open cafe. As per usual, the lady serving is grumpy, from boredom I reckon. On top of her grumpiness, she had no food, and a choice of Nescafe Coffee, or Nescafe Coffee. I bought one, just so I could sit inside and defrost, but I couldn't face drinking it, and then I dragged myself back out into the freezing bleakness. I'm in a "fug". I'm not smiling, I'm feeling depressed, and I'm thinking of the 30°C summer day happening at home in North Canterbury.

Some of the youngsters at the hostel were in a "fug" as well. When I arrived on Christmas Eve (2pm), some were just getting up for breakfast. They sat around until 10pm, and then hit the town. Christmas morning, they rolled into the dorm at 4am, and stayed in bed until late afternoon. Christmas Day, they were out on a pub crawl from 10pm again, and rolled in about 4.30am, straight from the Strip Club. Boxing Day didn't really happen for these guys. They were deep in "fug", especially the one who realised mixing with the stripper had cost him $500. One of the others didn't emerge from his bunk all day. The dorm smelled like a teenager's bedroom, fuggy to the max or what? (Their idea of travelling the world is slightly different to mine). Luckily, I was able to climb out of my fug.

10kms past the "no food cafe", the fog suddenly disappeared. What an amazing difference. I haven't really seen much of Bulgaria, through the fog, but here, it was very, very pretty. My spirits lifted with the scenery, and the road started to descend through a beautiful conifer forest, all the way to the Serbian border. I'm in the sun, I'm going downhill, and the fug disappears.

A Bulgarian exit stamp and a Serbian entry stamp took about ten minutes. It makes me think of the three and a half hour crossings in Central Asia. So quickly, I'm in country twenty-two, and it's amazing. The first village is old world Europe. Cobbled streets, bakeries, small shops, horses and carts filled with hay, and thatched roofs. I'm following minor roads through the villages, and dogs are not chasing me. I'm smiling. I'm having fun. And I see my first cycle tourer since central Turkey.

SWINGS N SEESAWS

29th December 2015

Perot Serbia to Predejane Serbia 90km
To Gjilian Kosovo 99km

Cycle touring in winter certainly plays with the mind. One minute you're up, the next you're down.

Cycling out of Perot, it was cold, it was foggy, but it wasn't nearly as dismal as the previous day. Perhaps because the traffic wasn't as heavy, and it wasn't long before I climbed out of the dense fog, and the sun started to break through, creating some amazing colours. The pretty little villages helped. And the descents into frosty valleys and gorges were pretty cool as well, with some of the streams frozen solid, and the road icy. For 60km it was "quality" winter cycle touring. I loved it.

Then today, more freezing fog, on a busy narrow road, being buzzed by big trucks, travelling far too fast for the conditions, and far too close to this unprotected cyclist, who is being sprayed by freezing road debris as they pass. I can definitely say "I was not in my happy space". Thirty minutes later, and I'm on the sunny side of the valley. It's dry, warm, the fog has disappeared, the trucks are on the motorway, and life is good, until the very scary tunnel, and emerging back into more fog.

I hid in a cafe for an hour to warm-up. A couple of local policemen came in. They were big burly chaps, very intimidating. They sat at the table next to me for their free coffee and food, and one started chatting to me, in good English. Turns out his intimidating looks are a charade. He reminded me very much of my mate Doobie. A lovely nature, interesting conversation, great smile and sense of humour, I just found it difficult to see past the big gun in his holster on his hip, remembering that it has been less than twenty years, since the people in this part of the world were slaughtering each other, neighbour vs. neighbour. As I cycled through the valleys, it was very apparent that some houses, and some whole villages, were abandoned, deserted, and unlived in. I tried to read up about the problems here, but the history and the story is very complicated. Albanians vs. Serbians, with religion thrown in, a slump in economy, wars in surrounding countries, the breakup of Yugoslavia, the fall of the Iron Curtain, all leading to some scary, very recent, conflict. It's all just a little unnerving.

So today, I passed into Kosovo. The border was quite busy, but I filtered up past the fifty or so cars waiting to cross and slipped into the queue just before the passport check. All very easy, until the Kosovo guard asked for my "vehicle papers"." What? For a bicycle?" He hadn't registered, because he was at a low desk, that I was cycling. He thought I was on a motorbike. Whew. There were heaps of Swiss cars in the queue. I'm sure they weren't too happy with my filtering. But the car with French plates happily waved me in front of them. I'm really feeling Europe now, as I spot so many different countries number plates.

There are lot of locals cycling in this part of the world, on old rusty single speeds, and modern expensive mountain bikes. But they all have one thing in common. The slightest hint on an uphill and they're off the bike pushing. It makes me feel great as I spin past young fellas, walking their bikes up a pimple.

The traffic in the cities that unexpectedly pop up, as they don't necessarily register on my map app is chaotic. The streets are narrow. Many are cobblestoned. Many are really rough cobblestone. Therefore, the traffic is really slow, so banks up. Vehicles keep joining and leaving the queues unexpectedly. No indication, no warnings, just a swerve in or out, with no regard for cyclists. Pedestrians have no consideration for cyclists filtering through traffic either. They continuously walk out in front of me, not even looking. I need to be totally awake and aware at all times. It feels so much like some of the Asian cities, chaotic traffic.

The festive season continues. It's 30th December, and as I cycled into the central square of Gjilian I can see four Santa's. They are being photographed with kids on their knees, as are the very good looking "Santa helpers", they are waving to traffic, with "Hohoho's", and dancing to very unChristmaslike music. There are still Christmas trees and decorations being sold as well. Perhaps it will stop tomorrow. As for me, I'm heading towards Macedonia. I'm sure it will be cold, probably foggy, with some warm sunny spots. That's if it doesn't snow. Back on the roundabout again.

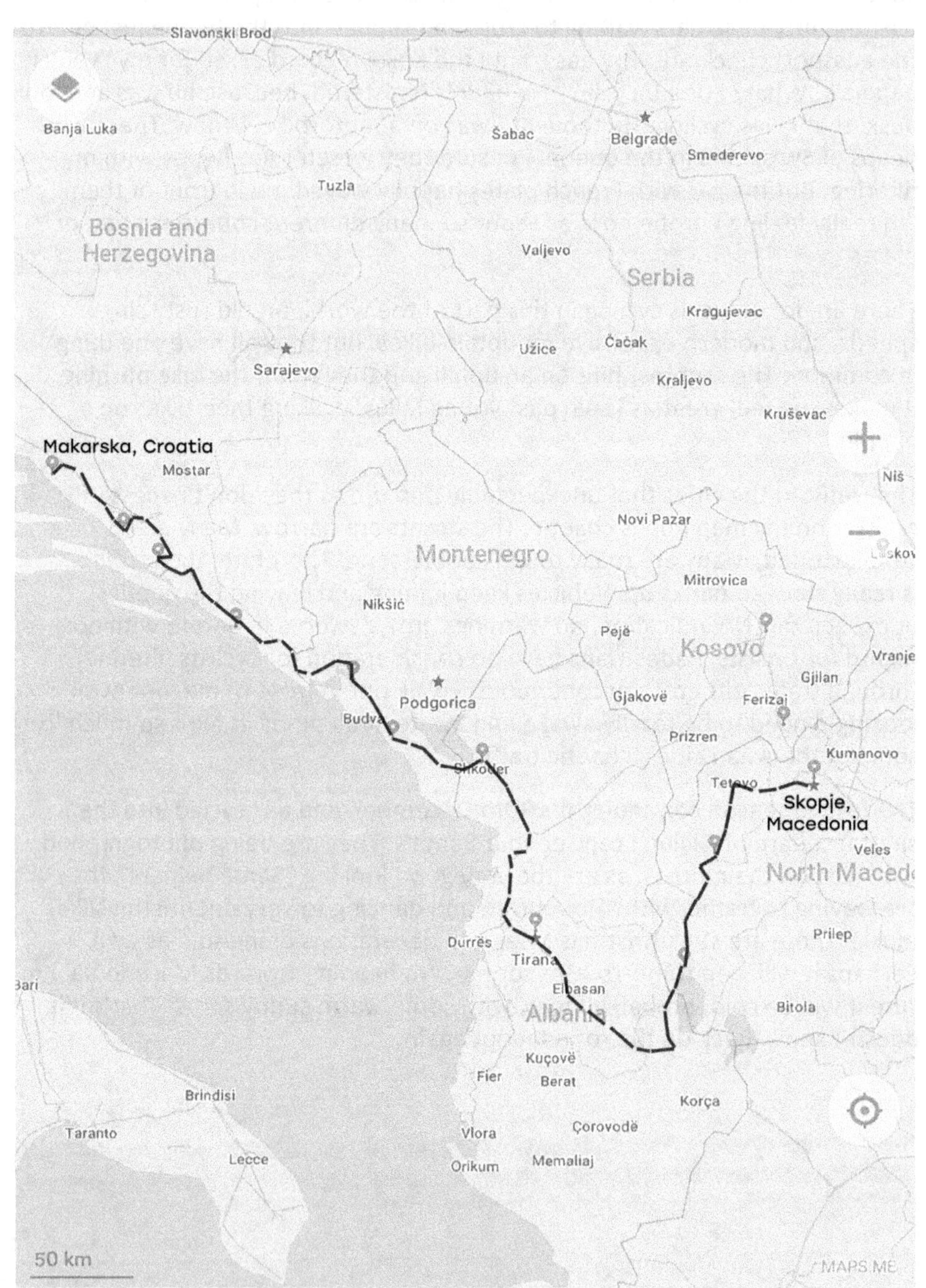

Slavonski Brod
Banja Luka
Šabac
Belgrade
Smederevo
Tuzla
Bosnia and Herzegovina
Valjevo
Serbia
Kragujevac
Čačak
Užice
Sarajevo
Kraljevo
Kruševac
Makarska, Croatia
Mostar
Niš
Novi Pazar
Montenegro
Leskov
Mitrovica
Nikšić
Pejë
Kosovo
Vranje
Gjilan
Podgorica
Gjakovë
Ferizaj
Budva
Prizren
Kumanovo
Shkodër
Tetovo
Skopje, Macedonia
Veles
North Maced
Durrës
Prilep
Tirana
Elbasan
Bitola
Albania
Kuçovë
Fier
Berat
Korça
Brindisi
Çorovodë
Taranto
Vlora
Orikum
Memaliaj
Lecce
50 km
MAPS.ME

A NEW YEAR

1st January 2016

Gilman Kosovo to Skopje, Macedonia, 83km
To Strazha Macedonia 77km

It's snowing as I cross the border into Macedonia. I've sifted past about fifty
cars, and the Kosovo border guard is very chatty. I'm not sure those I've past
are impressed, but I am. He asks me questions about my adventure, wishes
me a Happy New Year, a safe journey, and invites me to return soon. The
Macedonian guard is not quite as talkative, but the whole process takes
less than ten minutes. For the next 10km, I recognise cars I sifted past in the
queue. Cycling, in this part of the world, is great for crossing borders.

I head into Skopje. I've got a hostel ear marked, close to the city centre. I
didn't know beforehand, but Skopje is the birthplace of Mother Teresa, hence
the name of the motorway, and the park, and the museum. The hostel is
small, and very cosy. The hot shower is amazing. I head out to explore before
it gets dark. I want to check out what's on and where, for tonight, New
Year's Eve. I make some enquiries. Nothing is happening, because tonight
is not New Year's Eve, its tomorrow, bother. But I see a market, lots of crazy
looking fireworks being sold, and I'm told not to photograph them. Someone
sets a few off in the central market, which gives me a big fright; idiots. I also
see heaps of statues, to Macedonian warriors, poets, artists, musicians and
writers, and lots of impressive buildings and a stage for tomorrow night's
celebrations. I eat pizza at an Irish pub. Unlike Bulgaria, where there is a
McDonalds, KFC or Burger King, on every corner, Macedonia has no such
shops. On corners here are casinos, and slot machine places. It's 6pm,
-8°C, and it's been dark for almost two hours. I head back to the hostel and
warmth.

The real New Year's Eve, and I'm out wandering about 3pm. The bars and
restaurants are packed. I sit in the "Square", and watch the world go by. Four
Santa's, with their helpers, Mickey Mouse, some Raggedy Anne Doll, and
others I couldn't identify, are doing a roaring trade in photos. It's a week
since Christmas. Christmas hats, flashing lights, balloons, candy floss, it's all
happening. The band turns up at dusk, 4pm, for a sound check. They're pretty
good but aren't playing until 10pm. That's a long time after dark. I don't know
whether I will make it.

The temperature has dropped. It must be -10°C. Most people are pretty well
rugged up, but quite a few "young things" are pretty much "'dolled up", ready

for the big night. They look pretty hot in their skimpy gear, but I hope they're heading for a warm bar, because it's bleeding cold. I don't see the band perform. It's too cold, and I'm asleep before 9pm. I do get woken at midnight by incredibly loud fireworks.

New Year's Day and I am heading out of the city on the Mother Teresa motorway. There's no other choice. It's very cold, but the sky is blue, and the mountains have fresh snow on them. I pass three sets of toll booths. I keep getting waved on through. I bought some new gloves and socks at the market. The gloves are fantastic. The socks not so great, but I'm climbing a hill, and sweating. I'm just worried about the downhill, because that's when you get cold. A sign at a garage tells me its -12°C. Just over the summit, I get a little wobble on. Bother; a puncture. I strip the tube out, but my hands are so cold, I can't find the cause of the puncture in the tyre. I decide to replace the tyre with one of my spares, as the current one has done close to 19,000km, and has a few gouges, while the spare has only done 12,000km. I get slime all over my hands. My hands freeze. Getting the tyre back on is rather difficult. I'm cursing and laughing. This is ridiculous, and now I'm really cold, and I've got downhill. Oh-oh. Finally, I get it all together. Yeeha, but I'm shaking with cold. Luckily less than 3km downhill, I find a Cafe with hot soup, and hot chocolate. Wow I needed them. I thaw out.

Back on the road, and its 2pm, and I'm starting a climb. You have to remember, it's dark at 4pm. It's slow, and the sun has dropped below the hills. There's snow on the ground, and I'm tired. I start looking for campsites, but there's not much choice. I'm starting to get a bit worried. I stop for some food intake. My water has frozen solid. My juice is like a thick slushy. My Snickers is frozen hard, and I can't feel my lips, they're numb with cold, so don't know whether I've got it in my mouth. I'm a little more worried. Then I see a flag, a beacon. It's either the summit, or a petrol station. I'm saved. In fact, it's both, plus a couple of restaurants. I pitch my tent in an unused beer garden and go into the cheaper restaurant and dry my soaked clothes in front of a fire. Damn, I'm cold. Two hours, lots of food, several hot drinks, and the clothes are reasonably dry. I'm knackered and am happy to crawl into my sleeping bag. At least it's downhill tomorrow. I'll be rugging up with everything I've got, if I survive the night.

FROZEN IN MACEDONIA

2nd January 2016

Strazha to Struga Macedonia 70km

Almost everything is frozen. My host tells me it is -25C. My back-brake cable is frozen, so no brakes for the downhill. My water bottles are frozen solid. They have expanded so much I cannot get them out of the bottle cages. The rivers and drains are frozen solid. My toes are not frozen. Three layers of Icebreaker are keeping them warm. My tent is not frozen, because I've slept under a gazebo. My clothes are mostly warm and dry, except my inner gloves, which were obviously not dry enough. They are now frozen. My food is frozen, bread, bananas, cheese, chocolate. I guess I'm leaving here hungry.

The good news is I'm going downhill, so no sweat that would freeze, although the roads are frozen and icy. I'm taking it easy, being very careful. The mountains are getting smaller, and the scenery is beautiful, and the roads are very quiet.

I find a cafe attached to a petrol station. I'm desperate for something hot. They do have hot chocolate, but no hot food. I resort to pre-packaged pastries; not so good. A local guy takes my photo. He is a councillor and wants to put it in the local paper. A lovely young post grad student, travelling with her parents chats to me. She gives me some delicious apple cake her mum made. The best I've tasted in a very long time. Everyone is interested in me. In most other countries, when I explain what I'm doing, and then tell my listeners that "I'm a little crazy", they laugh and agree. In Macedonia, they disagree. They tell me I'm doing a great thing. A truck driver says "No. You are the intelligent one. No one stuck in an office at home will be seeing or experiencing anything like you. Not any time in their lifetime." I tend to agree.

I have a choice. I can turn left and go to a historic village for the night, and then circumnavigate Lake Ohrid to Albania, or turn right to Struga, stay there the night, before heading to the closer border. I'm knackered. The cold has taken a lot of energy. I head to Struga. The hostel I was counting on is locked up solid, but I find a hotel, and defrost.

I'm up early for breakfast. It's raining heavily. My host tells me it is very cold. I look out the window. The rain is freezing as it hits the ground. Apparently, it will be better and warmer tomorrow. I don't take too much convincing. I go back to my room. Eating, snoozing, and watching the Fox Movie channel. Before I know it, it's dark again. Days are short in Macedonia.

ALBANIA

4th January 2016

Struga to Tirana Albania 122km

It's a balmy 4°C as I leave my hotel in Struga, and I realise I've got too many layers on. I strip one off, and immediately start a 15km climb, into the snowy mountains, to find a border post on the ridge between Macedonia and Albania. It's snowing, familiar, so the layer goes back on.

In 1979, Eileen and I sailed past Albania, on a ferry between Italy and Greece. Albania was the first country I'd ever seen, that would not permit me to enter. Albania was locked tight. As I watched it slide past, a hunger to return and explore this hidden country developed. Thirty something years later, I enter Albania.

I'm on a windswept, snowy ridge, with very little vegetation. To my left, way below is a huge lake. To my right, even further below, is a town, hidden amongst clouds. Wow. This feels so like Central Asia. I begin an amazing descent. It's raining, so my glasses fog up, and I can't see a lot. But it's better than a couple of days ago when my breath had frozen between my corrective lenses and sunglasses, and there was a layer of ice on the rim of my helmet, frozen breath. Today it's only rain. I can choose between foggy view, with glasses, and blurry, distorted view without. I choose the second option.

The view as I descend is amazing. It feels like another world, and I'm not cold. The similarities with Central Asia continue as I enter the first town. The centre is abuzz with local men "hanging out". The predictable, unpredictability of the Mashuka, buses and taxis is all so familiar. I stop and ask a guy where I might exchange some money. He leads me to the back of the crowd of milling men and introduces me to a well-dressed elder man. This guy produces a small calculator, shows me the exchange rate, and brings Euros from one pocket, Albanian from another. I've got no idea, so trust he will not rip me off too much and accept a handful of notes. Great; now I can at least buy something warm to eat and drink.

The road drops away in front of me. My gloves are soaked, my raincoat and rain trousers (that have only been used once before) are soaked, but I love the ride. I'm not cold. Although it's winter, the colours of the dead leaves still clinging to the trees are outstanding. More Central Asian memories, as I see donkeys being used for transporting grass, hay and firewood, goats and sheep being herded, and horse and carts carrying whole families.

The crazy driving is so familiar, passing on blind corners, passing three abreast, double and triple parking. But they are all very courteous to this cyclist. People are calling out greetings, waving, tooting "Hello". I've missed this in recent countries.

I'm following an in spate river. It looks pretty boatable, and fun. The road and river are following down a gorge. Less than 50m in front of me, I hear a roar. I look up to see a landslide coming down towards the road. My brakes are not frozen. I'm able to stop in time. I wait for things to settle, and weave through the rubble almost completely covering the road. It may be a while before regular vehicles get through.

I see a sign, 45km to Tirana. 50m later there is another one, 51km to Tirana. I stop at the junction and ask. "It's 45km if you go on the motorway, and through the tunnel. It's 51km on a steep windy road if you go the non-motorway option." "Am I allowed on motorway on bicycle?" "No problem." No choice really then. 1km along the motorway, a huge sign tells all what the speed limit is for various vehicles. Down at the bottom, in the small print, it says no horses, no bicycles. I choose to not see the small print.

It's a long slow climb, but I'm well away from the zooming traffic. Eventually I reach the tunnel entrance. There is only one open lane, and there's quite a bit of traffic, no problem. I cycle in the closed left lane. I'm out of the way, I'm safe, and can easily skirt any hazard that has closed the lane. There is no hazard. After the tunnel, the motorway finishes. It's still raining, it's still mostly downhill, and I'm buzzing; the euphoria of breaking the law and not getting caught?

It's dusk as I enter Tirana. I have to find somewhere I can keep my phone screen dry, so as I can navigate to a hostel. Not easy when it's torrential rain, but weaving through narrow streets, filtering through traffic, going down one-way streets the wrong way, and dodging the Mashuka is pretty fun. The hot shower and being in dry clothes is even better. Tirana was where Ju was going to meet me for our European ride together. She's not here because I'm a month early, but it's pretty exciting to finally, after thirty-seven years, or nineteen months of cycling, to have ticked another box. And Ju will be in Rome.

IT'S RAINING, SOOO?

7th January 2016

Tirana Albania to Shkoder Montenegro 94km
To Canj Montenegro 61km

My "sometime cycle tourist" friend, an Irish Maths teacher, in the hostel tells me "on a wet day like this, I would put my bike on a bus. You're a bit crazy, aren't you?" My other new friend, a young Indian statistician, working for Rolls Royce in Norway, is excited that I am heading out into the storm. I'm really comfortable about my decision to get back on the road. It's not cold, only wet. I've had a day hanging, looking for sights, reading, resting, and now I'm restless. There's stuff to see so I've gotta go see it.

And it's wet, very wet. But I've got far fewer layers on, and I'm comfortable. The road is mainly flat, and not too busy, although there are places where it is underwater. I've probably not seen as much water since the drowned rice paddy fields of SE Asia. At times, I'm forced to ride through puddles, up to Fiona's hubs. The kilometres zip by. Unlike the mountains when I first entered Albania, these flat lands feel very European. At least half of the cars are Mercedes, the rest are BMWs or VWs. They are all reasonably new. The people seem reasonably well off, but I'm still dodging dodgy Mashuka.

A car stops in front of me. The driver owns a hostel in Shkoder and invites me to come and stay. She is accompanied by a young German cycle tourist who is spending January at her hostel, waiting for his cycling buddy. Sounds like a deal to me. She's even got a clothes drier, which I'm going to need. Initially I'm the only guest, and after I'm dry, am invited into the owners flat for bread and tea, very hospitable. Later, two Finnish girls arrive. They are interpreters, being able to speak twelve different languages each. To me, with my scant knowledge of only one language, English, this is amazing. And they make a living from these amazing skills.

The next morning, for the most, the rain has gone. I follow the main road towards the border. But it is such a small, quiet road; I'm not convinced I'm going the right way. Then around a corner, the border post. But this one is slightly different. There are three cars in front of me. A border official comes out and collects all of our passports. He tells me to cycle up a ramp. I watch as he scans my passport, and then tosses it through a window into another room. He waves me forward. Another guy is scanning my passport. Why? He stamps it, opens his window: "Welcome to Montenegro." Wow. That is efficient. I'm in country number twenty-seven.

And the changes are yet again apparent. The road is smoother. The houses look wealthier. The first three people I see speak good English, and all welcome me to Montenegro. I climb up a slight hill for a few kilometres, on a narrow country road between olive trees and stone walls. It's almost single lane and the traffic, the very occasional Mercedes, is travelling very sedately. This is great, and at the top, a beautiful panorama of a typical Adriatic city, sitting on the beautiful Adriatic coastline; stunning. I've heard about it. I've seen photos. And here it is, below me. Damn. I wish Ju was here to share it with me. She was going to join me for this section of my adventure.

Heading downhill and two cyclists on mountain bikes are racing up the hill. They stop, and we chat. They are Russians, living in the local city for two months, training. *"For what?"* Olga is the Russian Mountain bike Orienteering Champion, training for the World Champs in Portugal. Pavel is the Russian Downhill Mountain bike Champion, and a top Enduro rider. They are staying at his parents Montenegro villa, where his parents are helping, by looking after their three-month-old daughter, while they train. Pavel has to continue training, while I'm invited to accompany Olga back to the villa for a cup of tea. We race downhill. It's fun, and Olga is surprised I'm keeping up, but it is downhill, and Fiona has a bit of weight on her.

At the villa, really a three bedroom flat above a beautiful Adriatic bay, I meet the family. Dad, Alexander, has a brother who is a Russian Ambassador, living in Sydney. Wow. I'm in impressive company, but they make me feel as if I'm the hero. Hmmmm? We chat, look at each other's photos, exchange contact details, drink tea, a very yummy local herbal brew, and eventually, I drag myself away. I don't go far. I'm entrapped by the amazing scenery. I find a disused quarry, with a view across a bay, and pitch my tent. Am I really here? I almost have to pinch myself to ensure it's real.

MEDIEVAL WALLED CITIES

10th January 2016

Canj to Kotor Montenegro 50km
To Dubrovnik Croatia 100km

I don't usually deviate off my route for tourist attractions, but I had been told by three different people that I should visit Kotor, and as it was only 4km from the main road. But as I turned off the main road, all I could see was a huge hill, with narrow winding roads. Hmmmm. What I couldn't see was a cool place to visit, nor the 2km tunnel going through the mountain, and emerging into a pretty amazing walled city. I guess it's part of history that NZers don't get to experience at home that makes seeing something like this so special. Staying inside the walled city, in a cool hostel, with a rabbit warren of rooms was cool as well. Exploring the city, climbing up to the castle, and descending an ancient road, it doesn't take much imagination to see knights, princesses and knaves, and the village idiot, wandering these streets in the XII century.

I've started staying in a hostel whenever I can. It's a way I can get to meet people. To be honest, I'm over long cold nights in my tent, and lonely nights in hotel rooms. It's great to have someone to chat with. This time I met a semi pro skate boarder from Brazil, and four young kiwis. What a delight. I yakked away like a demented squirrel. Two medical students, and two physical education students, and two of them were the grandchildren of NZ Phys Ed guru Bob Stothart. It's a small world.

The ride out of Kotor was impressive as well. The road follows around the coast of a fiord like bay, passing through quaint seaside villages. It was pouring with rain, but there was hardly any traffic, so the cycling was nice, and once I got out of the bay, the weather cleared. Then I started a long slow climb, to a border post: stamp. I'm in Croatia.

I didn't realise that Dubrovnik Old Town was another walled city. The road climbed above the city for the last 4km, so the view was pretty cool. I had ear-marked a couple of hostels in the old city. My map didn't indicate that the city had heaps of steps, not easy with Fiona and a trailer. I got lost in the maze of streets, trying to avoid the steps, to find that all four hostels were closed for the season. Bother. But I did get to see lots, and I found out that this is where the Game of Thrones is filmed. It's amazing what I stumble upon in my ignorance.

So, I'm in an apartment. It's cheaper than a hotel, even though I'm by myself. This place must be a mad house in summer. There are hundreds of accommodation and eating places, but many of them are closed for the winter. I'm happy to wander around without the crowds. Today, wandering the walls of the city, I met a lovely Greek Pharmacist, who has been on a four day 'team bonding' weekend. We didn't realise we were meant to have paid to be up on the walls; Oooops. We decided not to bother finishing the loop after we got caught without a ticket.

The loyalties and affiliations of the people living in this region are really complex. According to Serbs, Kosovo people are crooks and Mafia. A flag I saw in Kosovo, flying everywhere, was in fact the Albanian flag, not the Kosovo national flag. Sarajevo, in Bosnia, is still really unsettled, with Bosnians, not mixing with the Serbs that live there, and some sort of separate, but unrecognized, state exists, within the city itself. I'm still confused where Herzegovina fits into the mix. Tomorrow, all going well, I will pass through the Bosnia Herzegovina access to the Adriatic Sea. It's a strip of land about 20km wide, surrounded by Croatia. Will I get my passport stamped?

THUNDER LIGHTNING & BROKEN CHAINS

13th January 2016

Dubrovnik to Ploce Croatia 102km
To Makarska Croatia 54km
To Split Croatia 64km

You wouldn't credit it, but sometimes the road along the Croatian coast is not very interesting, so I mix it up. Whenever I can, I head down to the coastline, and follow the minor, minor roads and tracks. There's no traffic, and often there are no people. The whole of the coast is closed, restaurants, hotels, and guesthouses, shops, shut up for the winter. The only people I see are tradesmen doing maintenance work.

Often there is a path right beside the sea. Sometimes it's like a Promenade, with closed bars, fast food and ice-cream stalls, and canoe rental outlets. It's pretty special having it all to myself. Of course, it's really nice when the sun is shining, but even when it's raining, hailing, and almost snowing, it's nicer than the highway. There are two things to be wary of, however. The route back up to the highway, when the path runs out, is often a real grunt; granny gear minus three. I've had to push up a couple of very steep climbs. The other thing is to remember to ask locals about the black dashed trail on the map and listen to their advice. Sometimes these trails can be four-wheel drive tracks. Sometimes they can be lovely single tracks, or sometimes they can be like today:

"Hello ladies. Can I cycle along this trail?"

"Yes, but not far. It turns to gravel."

"No problem."

"Then it gets very narrow, and steep."

"Could you mountain bike on this trail?"

"Yes."

"No problem then." That was a stupid, macho, BS reply. For half of the trail you could ride a mountain bike if you were as strong and skilful as World Champion Anton Cooper. The rest was a nightmare. Anyone who would even contemplate riding a fully loaded cycle touring bike, pulling a trailer, needs their head read. Let's just say it was an adventure, and blood was shed. I

walked most of the trail twice, once with Fiona, and once with the trailer. Other parts I walked three times, carrying the panniers on the third trip. At one stage, when I was unlinking the trailer, Fiona let me know she was sick of it, and tried to jump off the trail. I managed to grab her back wheel. Picture standing on a very narrow, loose and rocky trail, 100m directly above a beautiful blue Adriatic Sea, with Fiona hanging from her back wheel in one hand, and the trailer trying to join her in the other hand. I had to laugh.

So even though it's fun being off the main road, it has its moments. But mostly, it feels like being on holiday. I'm having fun, I'm smiling lots, and I'm being challenged.

Farbod, an Iranian American, and Antej, a Bosnian American were being challenged as well. I met Antej on a bridge. "Hi. Where you from? Where you going? You don't have a spare chain, do you?" "Nope. But I can fix a chain." A look of delight, as he doesn't have to cycle 30km to the closest bike shop. Farbod is on a rental bike. They've cycled from Bosnia to stay in Antej's father's RV, just an over-nighter really. They've got very little gear, and no tools, and a pump that doesn't work, and the broken chain is very dirty. "Okay. I'm not touching that horrible gunky mess. Here are the tools and a link. This is what you have to do." Two very happy American boys shout me dinner in a restaurant. And it's got beds available. The lads head off to their RV, and I head upstairs, my good deed done, and an invite to stay with them in Washington DC when I get there.

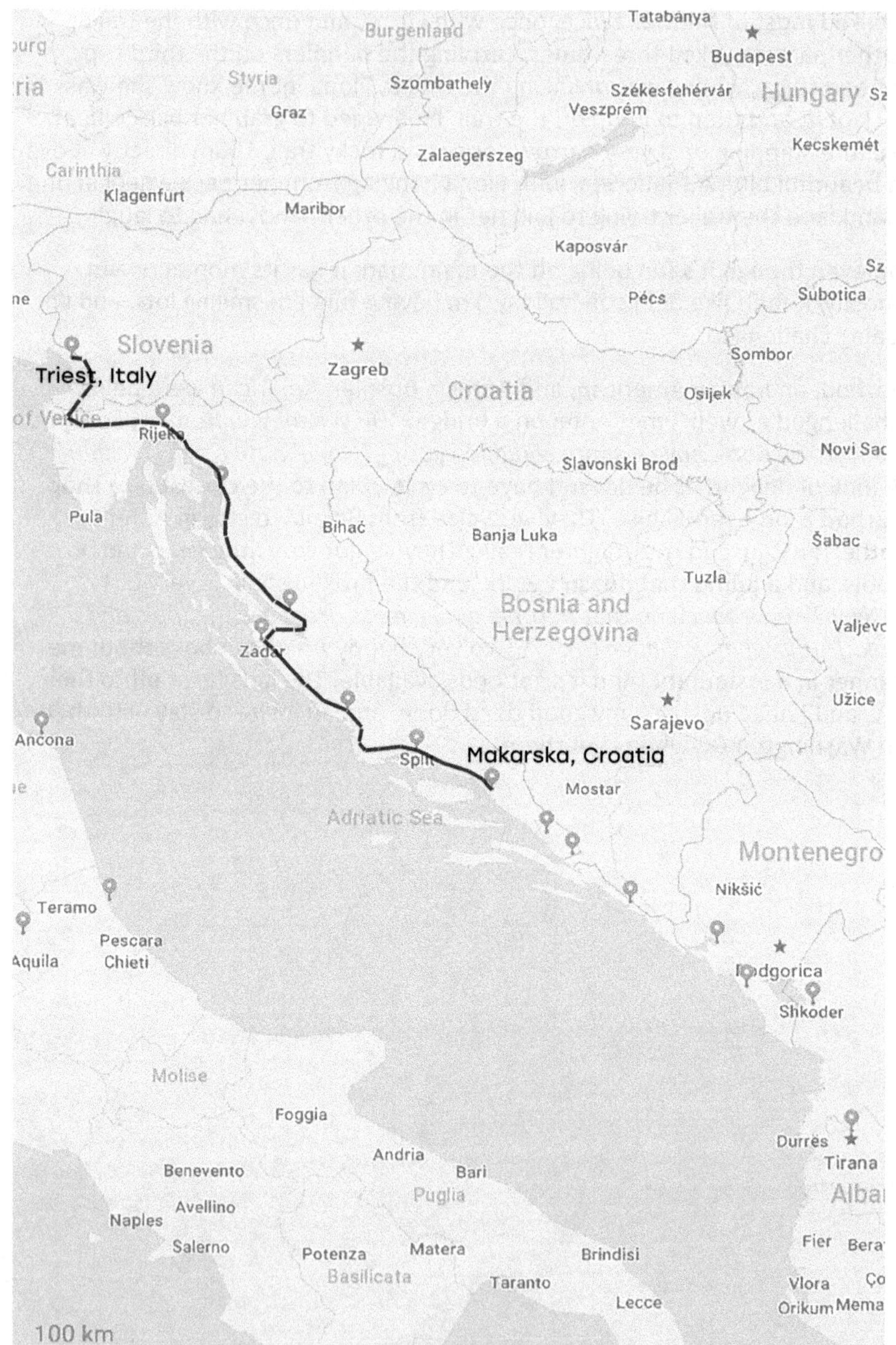

Tatabánya
Budapest
Burgenland
Styria
Szombathely
Székesfehérvár
Hungary
Sz
Graz
Veszprém
Zalaegerszeg
Kecskemét
Carinthia
Klagenfurt
Maribor
Kaposvár
Sz
Pécs
Subotica
ne
Slovenia
Sombor
Triest, Italy
Zagreb
Croatia
Osijek
of Venice
Rijeka
Novi Sad
Slavonski Brod
Pula
Bihać
Banja Luka
Šabac
Tuzla
Bosnia and
Herzegovina
Valjevo
Zadar
Ancona
Užice
Sarajevo
Makarska, Croatia
Split
Mostar
Adriatic Sea
Montenegro
Nikšić
Teramo
Pescara
Podgorica
Aquila
Chieti
Shkoder
Molise
Foggia
Durrës
Andria
Tirana
Benevento
Bari
Alba
Avellino
Puglia
Naples
Fier
Bera
Salerno
Matera
Brindisi
Potenza
Vlora
Ço
Basilicata
Taranto
Lecce
Orikum
Mema
100 km

DUCT TAPE & ZIP TIES

20th January 2016

Split to Sibenik Croatia 88km
To Zadar Croatia 48km
To Starigrad Croatia 76km
To Senj Croatia 115km
To Rijeka Croatia 67km

Two days of loud rolling thunder, followed by illuminating lightning, were pretty scary, and to be honest I was wondering just how safe it was being on the road. But there isn't too much choice, when so little is open, so I kept cycling. Then, overnight, the cloud and rain disappeared; the sun was shining, the sky a brilliant blue, and the wind started, from the north, freezing, and right on my nose. For two and a half days I cycled straight into it. But then I had to stop. They have closed the road in front of me, as the wind is too dangerous for vehicles. Yep, It was, once again, a bit scary. I was regularly walking across the viaducts and bridges because I wasn't feeling comfortable about where the next gust would deliver me.

It's no wonder that some of my stuff is wearing out; 600 plus days, and just over 33,000km, in all weathers. I'm so pleased I have my trusty 'fixers', duct tape and zip ties. I've got one or the other, and sometimes both holding together my shoes, my flags, my helmet, patching holes in my panniers, my clothes and my dry bags. They are wonderful tools and a must, on an adventure like this.

I was cycling towards Zadar, as I had been invited to stay with Warmshowers hosts, and what a delight it was. After several days staying in empty hostels, I had company, someone to talk to, in a warm, cosy, lived in Croatian home, amazing. They served a delicious homemade meal, including a traditional (vegetarian) meal, with mashed potatoes; oh, my goodness, bliss. And, despite my normal - "I'm over looking at old buildings and broken stuff", I was taken on a tour of the old city of Zadar, after dark. It's amazing how much more interesting a walk around a town can be, when you've got a guide who knows his stuff. (Hmmmm lesson for when I'm guiding.) Zadar Old City was extensively bombed by the Allies in WWII, trying to dissuade the occupying Italians. Close to 90% of the city was ruined, but this has allowed some cool stuff to be done.

Along the waterfront they have installed pipes. The waves flow through the pipes, creating an organ that produces music, twenty-four hours a day. I'm sure local residents do get used to it. As the restorations have been worked on, all sorts of ancient remains have been unearthed. A 'pillar of shame', ancient arches, and mosaics, all very interesting.

Best of all, when being hosted, is that I get so many questions answered. History, geography, tourism, outdoor activities, and politics were all discussed. Now here's something to get your head around. My host's grandmother has lived in the same village almost her whole life. During that time, if she had wanted, or been able to travel internationally, she would have had five different countries passports, The Kingdom of Yugoslavia, Austria, Italy, The Republic of Yugoslavia, and Croatia. We in NZ have had it so easy.

When the road was closed, I found myself at a hotel, at the doorway to Paklenica National Park. Even though it was extremely cold, I decided to have an explore. Paklenica is a very well-known area for its amazing rock walls, apparently the highest in Europe, up to 300m, and in the summer is busy with rock climbers from all over the world. This whole coastline of Croatia is amazing for adventure activities. I can see myself really enjoying the sea kayaking, the sailing, the mountain biking, the hiking, and even some of the alpine stuff available, and watching, in awe, the crazies climbing the massive walls. It is certainly worth a visit, but come in spring, summer, or autumn, when the weather is a bit more accommodating.

The wind has stopped but may start again (it's an annual occurrence), and so I'm making a dash for the next town. I heard its 104km. Damn, the extra 10km were tough, but the coast road was great. Fantastic views across the numerous islands, and tiny villages, tucked into tiny bays, protected from the horrendous January winds. I get to Senj, knackered, but the only hotel is closed.

Never mind. My host at the only open restaurant has a friend. A dodgy looking guy, leather jacket, and racey car, zooms me through a maze of streets to an apartment. It's not touristy. It's an apartment in a Soviet style apartment block, surrounded by scruffy kids, and cars on blocks. But it's warm, comfortable, and has a hot shower, and way too expensive. I accept. He zooms me back to Fiona. Trouble is, can I remember how to get back to the apartment. I make a couple of small navigation errors, but eventually find the correct building. Now, which floor was it on? Eight flights of stairs, hauling Fiona, plus panniers and trailer and I'm exhausted.

ITALY

RIDGES OR BRIDGES

23rd January 2016

Rijeka to Miramar Italy 89km

If given a choice, I would choose to cross a border across a bridge rather than a ridge, but usually there is no choice. Today was another ridge crossing, between Croatia and Slovenia. When I entered Croatia from Montenegro I had climbed to a ridge, and today was the same, up, up, up, and some more up, and it was cold, bitterly cold, and snowing.

My body has its own built in thermometer. My sinuses run like a tap when it gets down to 5°C. The fingers on my left hand go numb, and then throb at 0°C. My left eye weeps at -5°C. My toes and nose freeze at -10°C. It all happened today. Yippee. And the locals, on the coast think it's cold when it's 10°C. They obviously don't come up here to the border and wander around outside their warm cosy car.

Today I crossed two borders. The second was a non-event, passing from Slovenia into Italy. No border guards. No police. No ferocious dogs. No heavily armed military personal. No officials at all, and no stamp in my passport. Just two flags and a sign - Italia. Now that's a first on this trip, and unheard-of further east. I'm in the EEC, the 'real' Europe, as distinguished in my Atlas at Primary School, and I don't even get a stamp.

I had spent the last two days resting, sleeping, eating (lots), and wandering the streets. I love the old cities, the mazes of narrow streets, twisting and turning. I especially love the ones with multiple levels, with lots of steps. They would be amazing for Street Orienteering events. I'm sure it's been done. I really enjoy just following my nose, exploring. I discovered a monastery, and a castle, high above the old city, and then some cool, almost forgotten alleys and stairs, took me back down to the back end of the city. No cars. No buses. Not even motorbikes or bicycles. Just kids playing in the streets, really close to the top of the steps, and mums hanging out washing, Grandpa walking the dog, Granny struggling back up the steps with the groceries, a few young things dressed up and heading out, and some tough guys off to cause havoc, and me. Just the way I like it.

I needed the break. I can tell, when by about 2:00pm I'm yawning, and in need of a nana nap. I took the nana naps and today, it paid off. I climbed for 30kms. It was too cold to stop for more than a few seconds, and without the two-day rest, I would have struggled. I started with only a couple of layers, but more were piled on as I got higher. The trouble is, when you climb you sweat, and when you stop the sweat cools - no, freezes you. And who would have thought I would not be looking forward to the downhill. Cycling downhill creates a wind-chill factor, as if it's not cold enough already. Down, down, down, down, into Trieste. I stop to check my map, and without the wind, wow it's actually quite warm. A flashing neon sign tells me it's 10°C, but when cycling, my eye is weeping, -5°C.

Yep, it's happened again. Even though I was only in Slovenia for 40km (sorry Slovenian friends. I need warm.) it's very different from the Croatian coast, which is rocky and scrubby. Slovenian fields are well groomed, and rock free. The countryside is undulating, and many fields have been ploughed, and then, crossing into Italy, forests, and then a huge downhill back to the coast and a big city. But all are similar as well. Suddenly big 'supermarkets' have appeared where there is lots of choice. Graffiti, some of it very elaborate, is everywhere. The cars are all smaller, and most, a good deal more modern. Yep. I'm in the 'real' Europe.

I find a hostel. This time I'm not alone. There are thirty Bangladeshi male students here, studying for three months. I'm the only European. They all want to ask me questions, but their English is poor, my Bangladeshi is non-existent, and their Italian has an incredible strange accent, I've got no show of understanding. They are impressed by my cycling here from NZ, and I'm told Guptil is a great batsman. Déjà vu India.

Schaffhausen
(Allgäu)
Salzburg
Burger
Zurich
Appenzell
Ausserrhoden
Innsbruck
Austria
Styria
Szo
Salzburg
Graz
Luzern
Zug
Glarus
Liechtenstein
Switzerland
Grisons
Carinthia
Klagenfurt
Maribor
Z
Wallis
Ticino
Bolzano - Bozen
Trento
Udine
Varese
Pordenone
Slovenia
Zagreb
Bergamo
Treviso
Trieste, Italy
Monza
Brescia
Vicenza
Novara
Milan
Verona
Padua
Venice
Gulf of Venice
Rijeka
Pavia
Piacenza
Rovigo
Pula
emonte
Alessandria
Ferrara
Bihać
Parma
Modena
Bologna
Ravenna
Genoa
Forlì
Zadar
Savona
San Marino
La Spezia
San Remo, Italy
Lucca
Prato
Ancona
Marche
Pisa
Florence
Ligurian Sea
Livorno
Tuscany
Arezzo
Adriatic S
Siena
Sp
Perugia
Umbria
Grosseto
Italy
Teramo
Viterbo
L'Aquila
Pescara
Chieti
Ajaccio
Vatican City
Molise
Latina
Foggia
Andri
Caserta
Avellino
Sassari
Naples
Salerno
Potenza
M
Basilicata
Sardinia
Tyrrhenian Sea
100 km
MAPS.ME

EUROS

26th January 2106

Mirimare to Portogruaro 109km
To Lido Di Venezia 65km

Today I reached the most northerly point of my global adventure cycle, turning south at Carviginano del Friuli, and hoping it might start getting warmer. My original plans, which included cycling through Pakistan over the Karakoram Highway, into China, took me a lot further north, through Poland, Estonia, Lithuania, Russia, and above the Arctic Circle in Finland, Sweden and Norway. The whole trip, NZ to NZ, was going to take four years and eight months, but Juliet reckoned that was just a little too long to be away. *"Cut it in half"* were her instructions, hence the 900 days I'm using as 'time permitted'. And she was right. I'm happy to be heading towards home after 600 days, and very happy not to be heading north at this time of the year. I want warm.

Wow it's great to be dealing with Euros. I don't fully understand them yet but skipping through ten countries in the last five weeks, each of them with a different currency, was a bit taxing on this ol' fellah. A guy I met in Turkey told me that I should make an effort to learn some basic words in each language of the countries I visit. Maybe; please, thank you, hello, goodbye. I told him that's okay if you're only visiting a couple of countries, but I struggle figuring out the money of each, so learning ten different languages would stretch me well beyond comfort, and brain power.

I'm feeling comfortable in Italy. Things feel familiar. Maybe it's because I've been here before, but so much of the language feels familiar. Pizza, spaghetti, macaroni, pasta, sushi, Guardia, vino, all roll off my tongue with ease. Delicious hot chocolate and fresh berry muffins roll across my tongue quickly. Fresh, crusty bread and thick pasta sauce add to my comfort levels. Yes, it feels great. Hmmmm, did you notice almost all of the things that make it feel comfortable and familiar are food? It's just a cycle tourist thing.

The cycling is fun as well. The traffic is considerate, understanding and patient with cyclists, and many small towns and villages have cycle lanes. Today, cycling along a narrow road, I heard the soft touch of brakes behind me. I looked and there, in a queue, waiting to pass me were five trucks, three buses and half a dozen cars. I stopped and let them pass. No swearing. No loud horn honking. No loud engine noises. Just friendly waves, and thank you toots as they all past. Yep, so far, I'm enjoying Italy.

I'm heading towards Venice, the back route, because the main road is a motorway. There are wonderful country lanes through vino country, alongside canals, mint cycling conditions. And then the separated cycle lanes through the towns, riding couldn't be better. I arrive at a ferry terminal. *"But sir, you cannot take your bicycle to Venice." "What?" "It is not allowed. You will be fined by the police." "What? But I have a reservation at a hostel." "No problem, but NO bicycle."* Damn.

Fiona and I are now staying at a Hotel on Lido Di Venezia, and not at a hostel closer to the island of Venice. It's going to be very strange seeing the sites of Venice without her. For so long I had pictured the photos…

SAN MARINO

31st January 2016

Lido Venice to Passo Pomposa 70km
To Rimini 103km
To Marenella 72km
To Ancona 60km

Yesterday I cycled across my thirty second country, San Marino, a very small independent republic, nestled in the hills in central, eastern Italy. I could have followed a dual carriage way into San Marino, but have been having so much fun on the smaller roads, I decided to follow some lanes which involved short, steep, winding roads, through beautiful countryside, past very posh homes, surrounded by vineyards, and small village churches. It's amazing how little off the main drag you need to go to see amazing stuff.

Cycling out of Venice had been the same. I followed some very narrow islands, between 100m and 200m wide, and seven kilometres long, hopping on ferries between islands. People live here, protected by a three-metre seawall in the east, and only as far as you could lob a tennis ball, just over a cluster of houses, is the west coast. I missed the first ferry by thirty seconds, but that's no problem, it comes every twenty minutes, except for this hour, it's sixty minutes, and the wind is cold. The second island seems a bit deserted. There is a sign at the ferry jetty, 'bicycles allowed at the Captains discretion, according to number of passengers.' It shouldn't be a problem, as there are only four of us. The ferry docks. It's chocka. It's Market Day in Chioggia, where I'm heading, and it seems the whole population is returning, stocked up with fresh vegetables and groceries. Luckily, I'm heading in the opposite direction.

Chioggia was amazing. It is a busy fishing port, with cobblestone streets and colourful fishing boats. The whole main street is blocked by the market, and not a tourist to be seen, just locals and me. I love it. I thread my way through narrow lanes to find a road that will take me along the coast.

I'm cycling along cycle paths that follow the beach. Everything is closed. There are bars with beach volleyball courts, and some sort of court that might be for some sort of bowls, but they're all fenced off and locked. It seems like it would be difficult getting to the beach in the summer without passing through these areas. Hotels are closed as well. I'm done for the day. The town I've arrived at has three hotels, a lot less than most. One has a 'Full' sign, but no sign of life. Another looks like it was abandoned years ago. The third wants me to pay $75.00 without breakfast. Nope. I call into a bike shop. The owner drags his elderly father out and instructs him to show me some B&Bs, on his E-bike. We visit six, but none are open. Bother. I cycle out of town looking for somewhere to camp.

It takes a while to learn how things work in each country you visit. In Iran, service stations serve petrol and diesel and nothing else. In Turkey they often have a reasonable supermarket attached, often a restaurant, and sometimes even rooms. In Italy many have a café/bar, so drivers can have a few quick shots, alcohol or coffee, and a large parking area for truck drivers to rest up. They're also happy for me to camp in a quiet corner. Great.

Many years ago, when my kids were about seven or eight, we were in Paris strolling the streets and stumbled upon a red-light district. The kids were fascinated by all the ladies "all dressed up but not going anywhere". I think we explained they were waiting for visitors. They might ask similar questions about the dressed up ladies standing at road junctions and waving at the truck drivers. They might also ask "why is that truck driver not turning off his motor in the middle of the night?" And "why have they left their balloons all over the car park?" My corner campsite wasn't as quiet as I thought it might be.

I'm following another coastal cycleway, and its weekend, with heaps of people out cycling, skating, walking and running. My tent, sleeping bag, and clothes are really damp from a couple of nights camping, so when I find a nice spot, with a bit of sun, and a breeze, I decide it's good for drying stuff out, and perhaps making camp. I usually try and camp discreetly, but sometimes it's impossible, so it's a balance between discrete and obvious. Tonight, I'm obvious, but as it gets dark, the cycle path and beach clear, and my campsite becomes discrete, with just the roar of the very speedy trains zooming past every twenty minutes or so. I crawl into my now dry sleeping bag. 10pm. A club opens up, about 100m up the beach. Beat box music. Loud. Until 4am. Then the party makers hit the beach. Luckily, I'm almost invisible in the dark, and I'm not disturbed. I get another couple of hours sleep, before the early morning fitness nuts start cycling, running and skating past.

TOWN, HILLS, CASTLE

2nd February 2016

Ancona to Mosciano 131km
To Ponte della Lama 62km

It seems that every town in Italy has a hill, or a moat, or is part of a harbour, and on that hill, or behind the moat, is a castle, a monastery, or some sort of church. I met an Italian guide the other day, and he told me how much he enjoys guiding in Italy, as every town has a story, and all sorts of history. I'm really enjoying cycling through it all as well. Sixth form history lessons coming to life. Unification of Italy. Garibaldi and his Red Shirts. I'm just sad that I know so little about so much of the history of SE Asia, India and Central Asia, because it certainly adds spice to your cycling.

Ancona has a nasty hill to navigate around to get out of town. Italians engineers are fantastic, engineering amazing tunnels, flyovers and underpasses, but if you're not allowed to cycle on them, it makes for some tricky navigation, avoiding 'no go' tunnels and motorways. Probably the most frustrating city I've ever had to cycle out of, and a very steep hill seemed to be the only option. Bother it.

But eventually I was again cycling along beach front cycle trails. They're magic. No traffic worries, just the odd Zimmer frame to dodge. There are not as many cyclists out today, being Monday, but those that are out, all seem to be grey bearded and wearing brightly coloured, tight fitting clothes. I fit right in and get lots of waves.

I saw some other interesting stuff as well. There are a lot of these big rat-like creatures, about as big as a cat. Saw some as roadkill, but also others grazing on the roadside. Can anyone tell me what they are? How about storks or cranes, the bird type, sitting on power lines. They look as if they're going to over balance, but also look very regal. And above ground graves. Buildings that look as if they have draws in the side, but they are actually graves.

The weather is so much warmer, so I've been camping. I was looking for a good place as I cycled along the beach. Yep, this looks like a possibility. Just have to wait for people to disappear, and for it to get dark. An old fellah on an ancient clanger, single speed, is taking an interest in me. After cycling past three times, I greet him in Italian. He stops and starts rattling on in Italian. I try to explain that I don't understand which does not dissuade him, but we do communicate. Basically, he tells me that if I'm cycling to Roma, I should have taken a turning 50km ago. I should not keep going to Pescara, but head inland now, *"Come on. Now. I will show you."* I reluctantly follow. He leads me three kilometers along back lanes and points, *"Roma that way"*, so much for a campsite by the beach. The third gas station I stop at lets me camp in a field behind them, away from the car park.

There's lots of snow on all the very high peaks in the west. Locals have been questioning my sanity, heading for Roma this time of the year. They tell me *"mountains, winter, cold, hilly road, snow."* I'm unsure about my own sanity, and wary of not taking local advice. I could take a train, or hitch a ride along the motorway, and through the massive tunnel. No stuff it. I've done mountains, winter, cold, snow and hills and I can do it again.

It's up, and up, and up. But its 15°C and sunny, and I'm climbing through a stunning gorge, with amazing scenery. There's very little traffic, perhaps four vehicles an hour. At one stage I'm cycling uphill, through a tunnel, with head wind. What? It's an old Roman road, glorious scenery and fabulous cycling. But by 3pm, I've done 60km, all of it uphill, and my legs are shot. It's time to stop.

I'm above the National Park boundary, and there are signs to beware of deer, roe and boar. There's snow in shady areas, and lots of choice for campsites. I get the camping gear out and stretch it all out to dry in the last of the sun and breeze. Can this really be a main road? In the two hours before dark, two cars pass by my campsite. As it goes dark, I erect the tent, and climb inside my sleeping bag. It has suddenly become very cold. I hope there's not too much more uphill. I'm short on food and water. Still, twelve hours sleep is going to do heaps for my recovery.

THIS ROAD LEADS TO ROME

4th February 2016

Ponte Della Lama to Rieti 74km
To Roma 80km

Five more kilometers uphill and my legs are really feeling it. Did I really just have twelve hours sleep? It feels like I haven't been off my bike. It's cloudy, but the all-night breeze has ensured the tent is dry for packing. I just hope it doesn't rain, or snow. And I need food and water. The cake I had for breakfast is not going to do my energy levels much good.

And then the downhill starts. Oh my, gloriously smooth Italian roads, sweeping endlessly downhill. In 20km, I pass two uphill vehicles. Any downhill traffic can't keep up. The pain in my legs disappears. Then a village. *"Is there a market (Supermarket)?" "Yes, 100m up there."* It wasn't even steep cobblestone, but it felt steep, and it was cobblestones. Outside the market was a guy selling fresh bread rolls, with pork or chicken. I'll have two of them thanks, and a litre of juice. A local guy joins me. He only has half a roll, with a glass of wine; it's 9am. He explains that one wine is okay, two not so good, three and he won't do any work today. He is fascinated with my journey. His buddy wants to see what kind of battery I have in the trailer. Not finding one they are amazed at how tough I am and decide on a second wine. They are enthusiastic and supportive, have lots of questions about my route, and decide on a third wine to celebrate, do I want one? But maybe not, as cyclists get breathalysed in Italy.

Oh bother, some more uphill. Only slight, but it hurts. And it heads up into the clouds. Damn. But mercy me, it is only for 5km, and it didn't rain or snow, and there before me is a long, long, deep valley. There's only one way the road can possibly go, down. And it does so for 30km. Bliss.

Italy is a pretty cool place to visit, but even better to cycle. There's so much to see. In the last forty-eight hours I've cycled through coastal towns and villages, up an amazing gorge, through a glorious National Park, and through fantastic inland villages, with really old buildings, and even past an old Roman stadium. Around every corner is something new to create interest and amaze that seems to call out, "Come and explore." Yep. I'm enjoying Italy.

I cycle into Rieti, looking for a hotel. The black clouds are looking threatening. There are three hotels on my map. The first is four stars, so way out of my price range, so I cycle away, and get lost in a maze of tiny alleyways and streets. My phone gets wet, and my map app won't work, bother. I stumble upon a three-star hotel. He wants $75.00 plus $10.00 to house Fiona. You've got to be kidding? I lose myself again. With some help I find the Blu. It's cheaper, by far. There are about thirty African men hanging out. They are all refugees and have just finished their daily Italian lesson. One helps me get registered, as he speaks English. He is Gambian. He has been in Italy 18 months, having travelled overland through Africa, then across the Mediterranean on a very decrepit boat. He's hoping for a better life, but can only get a car washing job, lowest pay scale, but he has no documents, a huge challenge.

Siesta times in Italy, anytime between 12:30 and 4:30pm. Don't bother trying to do anything. The whole country closes down, except for the tradesmen, who work on through, 'salt of the earth'.

Freezing rain overnight, so I'm glad to be in a hotel, and there's a very cold wind blowing as I set off, but it's a tail wind, behind me all the way to Rome, woohooo. Traffic and navigation in the city itself, was not as easy, but I'm here. 34,000km from home, in Roma, waiting for my lady, and some romance. And sorting my USA visa.

TRAINS, BUSES AND TRAMS

17th February 2016

Zagarolo

Today, I picked up my USA visa. It has been a long journey. I needed to apply for a six month visa, rather than the usual three month waiver, if I was going to be able to cross the USA at a reasonable pace, and not have to race against the calendar. To do this you have to make an application online, and then visit an USA Embassy for an interview.

I began the process in a hostel in Osh, Kyrgyzstan, way back in July. My plan at that stage was to have the interview in Lisbon, Portugal, and as the availability of Wi-Fi through Central Asia and Iran was at that point unknown, and I was having a few days' rest, with excellent Wi-Fi, I took the opportunity. The form you fill in is not simple, especially on a Samsung Notebook, and it took me a couple of long days, gathering all the information I needed. Thankfully, it was here I met an American lad who offered to be my USA referee. Thus, the application was submitted.

Then plans changed. I crossed Central Asia and Iran quicker than expected, which meant that meeting Juliet in Albania wasn't going to fit in with her holiday dates. How about we meet in Rome? Now that called for some thought. Getting my visa in Rome would allow me to buy cheaper airline tickets to New York, being able to buy them earlier. One of the instructions on the visa application is "Do Not Pre-Buy Tickets to USA". But surely, I could get to Rome in time to get the process completed before Ju arrived.

Yep, I did it, and en route I followed up the application. Rome meant some more paperwork, and payment, either bank transfer, from an Italian Bank (I don't belong to one), or Debit Card (the one I left NZ with has lapsed, and the NZ bank would not let Juliet register a PIN number for my new card, because it's Not Her Card). With only hours left before the whole application would void itself, Juliet was able to pay with her card, from Christchurch. Phew.

Interview day and I'm lined up at 10am for my 10.15am appointment. At 11.15am I checked through security. At 11.45am I'm called to the desk. They can't find my application. It needs to be transferred from the Lisbon Embassy files, but it's not working. 12.15, and still nothing, and the Consulate is closing for lunch. I need to come back at 2.30pm. I'm first in line, because I lined up at 2pm, and get through security by 2.45pm. Woohooo. They've found the application. The lady is very interested in my plans, and we chat, and then I'm summoned by the Consul.

"Why do you need more than the 90-day waiver?"

"Where will you be staying?"

"How will you finance you trip?"

"Okay. Visa is granted. Pick it up from DHL in four days."

Woohooo.

So, I decide to get out of the bustle of Rome for a few days, and cycle out, and get sick, and have been recouping at Zagarolo Wiki Hostel. But today I could go and pick up my passport. I'm not up to 30km on my bike, so the other option is public transport.

The first leg, into central Rome Is by train. At 9am, it's only a small train, and it's packed, and stuffy, and hot and smelly, and it's winter. I'm struggling to breathe and trying not to cough over everyone. Thankfully, it's only forty minutes, but by the time we arrive, I'm feeling pretty wasted; still no time to waste. I need to get to DHL before they decide to close for a siesta. I need to find Tram number 14. It's pouring with rain, but I dodge the worst, and jump on the tram just before it leaves. I hope it's going the right way. Twenty-one stops and I have to get off, did I count correctly? The tram is packed solid, and I can't see the street or stop names. I take a gamble. Yes, got it right. Next, bus number 508. Ten buses come past before 508. Let's hope I can count the fourteen stops. Yes. Nailed it. Now it's a 1km walk, and the DHL office is still open. Yeeha. It's taken just over three hours. It takes less than five minutes to sign for my passport, and then I get to reverse the process. Six and a half hours on public transport. I'm knackered. But I've got a six-month visa for the USA, valid for ten years. Now that's got to be worth the effort.

I can book some flights. I want to fly from Lisbon to New York, but the flights I've found will not allow me to carry excess baggage. So, I've booked flights from Madrid, and will go from Lisbon to Madrid by train. Well I tried to book them. Got everything sorted, until the payment, and the NZ bank told me I was using the wrong PIN number. I don't believe it. Luckily, the booking saved itself long enough for Juliet to pay with her cards. I'm going to have to give her some very special hugs when she arrives on Saturday.

I will leave Madrid on 29th April and arrive in New York on 30th April. The plan is to cycle down the East Coast to at least Winston Salem in North Carolina, and then head west across the South to Austin, Texas, then north to Denver, and Salida Colorado, south, to Durango, and Flagstaff, Arizona, and west to San Diego. Who's coming?

I'M JUST NOT A GREAT TOURIST

20th February 2016

Rome

I knew five minutes into our three-hour guided tour of the Vatican that I wasn't in the right place. Ju had booked the tour from NZ. It's something she'd always wanted to do. Last time I had been in Rome I'd deliberately worn shorts so as to be rejected at the door. This time I was in longs, and I got to hear about the Cardinals, Bishops, Priests, Painters and Pope's who have lived here for 1000 years. It all went over my head, except the part where one Pope cut off the genitalia of all the naked statues. My eyes watered. At least we were part of a small group and were able to sneak past the huge queues. Wow. This is the off season and it was crowded. I'd hate to be here in July.

I really enjoyed the stroll back to the hotel, following our noses through narrow streets, and happening upon interesting piazza and activities. Not for me the following of the tourist's bible, the Lonely Planet.

I had deliberately got out of Rome after getting my USA visa. I wanted to share the sights with Ju, and I needed to get away from the crowds. The plan had been to visit Cassino, as the 18th February was some sort of anniversary of NZ troops fighting there. But I got sick and stumbled upon the Wiki Hostel. What a fortuitous find. It was so relaxed; quiet, with lovely staff, and in a lovely setting. And only minutes' walk from an ancient city, which was tourist free, and from a railway station, if you really needed to visit Rome. There were only a few guests, but they were all interesting. The Canadian teacher on half term break from her Windsor school, the German musician, who spoke unaccented English, having a week away, and the Mexican, and Italian, and English, and Austrian volunteers working at the hostel.

But the highlight of the week, no the month, nope the last several months, was meeting Ju at the airport. It's amazing how fast the last months, that I've been counting down, have gone, compared with the time between her plane landing, and the lady herself appearing through immigration, but I was still smiling. I knew she had bought me Marmite (and bike parts, and Squirt Lube, and new glasses from Shattky's and new ExPed mattress from Bivouac Outdoor). But she was knackered. Thirty plus hours flying can do that. We spent the next three days seeing Rome, and I was smiling the whole time, because I got to share the experience.

Fiona went in for service. Ju's bike got rebuilt. We ate at expensive pizza restaurants. Ju drank wine. We stayed in a nice hotel, with pleasant staff. Then we jumped on our bikes and rode through the morning traffic, until we found a cycle way along the river Tiber that took us out of the city. Our first day on the bikes, following a busy country road, up along a ridgeline, with amazing views over surrounding valleys, and hilltop villages, ended with an adorable campsite next to a river. I'm back doing what I really enjoy, and I'm sharing the experience with someone I love. Yep. I'm smiling.

BLOSSOM RAIN & MUD

27th February 2016

Roma to Gallese Teverina 82km
To Pianlungo 76km
To Ronzano 79km

For the last two months I've been cycling in temperatures between 10°C and -10°C. The first day that Juliet cycles with me in Italy, it is 25°C. She really is a ray of sunshine. Not only is it warmer, but there are trees in blossom. Now that's got to be a good sign. But we forgot what else spring weather is known for, rain.

After camping on the edge of a cycle track, next to a river, on night one, we continued along beside the river, and them on to narrow country roads. We have been invited to stay with friends from NZ, in a villa, Tuscan Sun Villa, about 150km up country, and especially for dinner on Friday night, so we've sat down and planned a route that keeps us away from motorways and other busy roads, and we're on a mission to get there on time. The route follows cycle paths, narrow country roads, and the occasional black dashed trail, which I had experienced in Croatia. These ones look reasonably flat and straight.

All is going well. It's fun navigating, the scenery is really pleasant. There's very little traffic. Okay, it's raining off and on. That's no problem. We've got the right gear. We turn on to the first black dashed trail. It's lovely, crossing through farmer's fields, close to rural buildings and houses. We greet locals working in fields and orchards. Juliet is happy. *"This is nice. I just didn't want to be riding on muddy wet single track."* BOOM. We turn a corner to find a wet, rutted, muddy, slippery hill. Oh bother. Within seconds Fiona's brand-new tyre treads are clogged with mud. Juliet's much meatier treads are also clogged. We are slipping and sliding uphill. There is totally no traction and we are off the bikes and pushing. *"I'm sure this won't last long."* (That was me) *"Or get much worse."* Ju reckons it was at least 5km, I reckon maybe 2km. And it did get worse. The ruts got deeper and wider, the mud thicker and more slippery, and it didn't help that some idiot had driven his tractor through the trail earlier that morning. The saving grace, was the knee deep river we had to wade through, to get to the gravel road at the end, which washed enough mud off the tyres that they were able to rotate.(Did I tell you how much I love my wife. She hardly complained.)

Okay; plan change. We are NOT going to cycle anymore black dashed trails. Ju is a little despondent. We've taken three hours to cycle less than 20km. She really wants to join our friends for the meal tomorrow night. The roads are still narrow, and wind across country, but they are hilly, and we are both weary. Pizza in a small village helps. Eventually we get to another village that we hope might have a hotel. It's raining heavily, with some hail. We are both very muddy, and a warm shower seems like a fantastic idea. No luck. The nearest accommodation is 3km in the wrong direction, or 7km up a hill. We cycle on.

Following our route are two railway lines. On our left is the local line, with slow trains that stop at every station. On our right is the fast train line. Every five minutes a bullet train screams past us. We're told they are travelling close to 250kph. We find a campsite. It's a little exposed, and close to a road, but the road is very quiet. It's about 200m from the fast train track. They are not quiet. But it's raining, and the sound of the rain on the tent, almost, somewhat muffles the roar of a bullet train through our tent every five minutes until late at night. Or not. Luckily, we are both very tired.

Day three out of Rome, and the route to Tuscan Sun Villa follows along quiet country roads beside a canal, after 15km of gravel uphill, and a lovely hilltop village, where we had great hot chocolate and pizza. Then, after finally some fun downhill we follow a cycle route, also along the canal. Initially it's really lovely, pleasant cycling, but the further along the trail we go, the less it has been used. The trail gets thinner, and the surface softer, and its hard going, even though it's flat. A huge storm is approaching, and we are both tired. We decide to get off the cycle trail and back onto the road. Oh bliss. The bikes are still caked in mud, but it seems so much easier. 10km later, we are climbing the last hill to Tuscan Sun Villa, and we've beaten the storm.

Our friends are not back from their sightseeing, but that gives us a chance to declog the bikes, and wash our panniers, under an outside shower. Then it was hot showers, and a wonderful meal, cooked by two chefs, who came to Tuscan Sun Villa specially to prepare the meal for us. I reckon we've earned a little bit of luxury, and it's fantastic to be sharing it with friends, but will I get Juliet back on her bike?

SIENA

29th February 2016

Ronzano to Siena 68km

A dream come true for Juliet, staying in a Villa in Tuscany, with wonderful people, drinking wine, and coffee (decaffeinated? Oooops), visiting hill tops villages, and eating wonderful food. She did not bounce out of bed in the morning, eager to jump back on her bicycle, in the pouring rain, and climb the hilly drive back to the main road. Oh well. She's on holiday. But the next day, even though it was still raining, we had to leave. Our hosts were off to Venice. Oh well. We'll be right.

Actually, it wasn't that bad, and we were pretty comfortable, until a motorist sped through a huge puddle and drenched us. Oh, and then we realised our planned route was actually a motorway, so no bicycles. So, it was a small backtrack, onto the smaller roads, which were really nice. Tuscany is beautiful. Amazingly green fields, old buildings, narrow streets and roads, and gentle hills, and it didn't actually rain too hard, if you don't mind dodging cats and dogs.

We arrived in the hilltop town of Siena mid-afternoon and found a hotel. A walk through the narrow streets, and we knew that we wouldn't have time to explore it all that evening. We booked an extra night. So, the kilometres in Italy are not flying past, but Juliet is having a wonderful holiday, and I'm very much enjoying sharing it with her.

A TUTU THROUGH TUSCANY

3rd March 2016

Siena to Toscana 84km
To Lucca 38km
To Sarvana 80km

The focus of my trip has changed somewhat. At the moment I seem to be 'cycle meandering' rather than cycle touring. My daily kilometre average has plummeted. Most nights are spent in plush (for me) accommodation. Meals are eaten at fancy restaurants. There's wine on the table every night. When walking though the ancient cities, I hang out in the shopping areas rather than the back alleys. I'm also hanging out, outside churches. To tell the truth, I am very much enjoying the change, because every moment is being shared with my wonderful wife. A guy in a cycle shop in Rome said to me, *"Mr, if you've got a wife who cycles with you, you are a very lucky man."* I've got to agree. I'm a very lucky, and relaxed, and happy man.

I do still ask questions though (in my head): *"Why do you have to go into so many shops?" "Because they're different from home." "Really?" "Do we have to visit so many churches?" "No, just most of them." "But this city, Lucca, surrounded by 3km of wall, has thirty-three churches." "Yep, but they're all different, and not like those at home." "Okay, I'll sit here in the sun, and watch all the good-looking Italian women walking past."* I'm happy.

When I was in Istanbul, and other cities in Central Asia, I was astounded at the number of mosques, on every corner. Here in Italy, I'm astounded at how many churches there are, once again, on every corner. It just goes to show how tight a grip religion has had on people, in all parts of the world, for such a long time.

Siena and Lucca, walled cities, both have over thirty churches within their walls.

The kilometres have dropped. We seem to find reasons to stop every three or four kilometres - photo, too hot, too cold, navigation - but the cycling still has lots of wow factor. We are riding through amazing villages, beneath huge churches and castles on hills, through amazingly green fields, and past colourful stands of trees and bush, and more often than not, on quiet winding roads.

Today, Saturday, we were greeted all day, by groups of cyclists out training. Then we turn down a straight road, between ploughed fields. Every 200m to 300m, there is a woman, sitting on a stool. It's a coolish, blustery day, with a storm threatening. There's a bit of traffic, but not much. There are no trucks, it's Saturday. What the heck are these women doing? This is not a bus route. There are no train tracks. They are not trying to hitch a ride. They have no vehicles or bicycles. There are no crops for them to guard, and no birds for them to scare away. Hmmmm. Mystery.

Woohooo. Today, we reached the western coast of Italy, which means I've cycled across the whole country. I get to add another sea to my visited list, the twenty-first, the Ligurian Sea. There is a huge carnival happening here on the coast. A rather rude security guard informs us, 'Closed', as we try to cycle down the cycle track. But oh dear, the weather is turning. We are cycling with a very strong tail wind. We venture out on to a pier, in the very strong wind. The Ligurian Sea is smashing it. It's scary standing above the huge unruly surf, but there are guys out surfing it, and having a ball kite surfing. A huge thunder and lightning storm catches us. We try to shelter, but I'm soaked. Ju is not so bad and is very happy with her new waterproof Endura shorts. We arrive in Savarna, meet our Warmshowers host, and luxuriate in a warm shower, and lovely company. Oh, my though. It's a very late night. Will I get Ju out of bed in the morning?

I'm very much enjoying this 'holiday'.

CINQUE TERRE

9th March 2016

Sarzana to Corniglia 47km
To Rapallo 61km

Cinque Terre, the Five Towns. Who's ever heard of them? Not me. But my adorable wife had, and she wanted to go there. So have thousands of other tourists, but thankfully most of them visit during the summer, although there are quite a few USA students, and some Asian tourists, and a few French about, but NO, ZERO, NADA, cycle tourists. In fact, we were told that only a macho madman would even consider cycling into Cinque Terre with a fully loaded tour bike. Bother. But it's a World Heritage UNESCO Site. Nope, you'd have to be bonkers. It's tough. People who visit this region, arrive by bus, car, train, or boat. NOT bicycle.

We had stayed in Sarzana, with another amazing Warmshowers host. He was full of advice and helpful suggestions, so we even stayed two nights so as we could visit another small coastal town, Porto Venere. On Monday we followed his directions, firstly to a Samsung shop. The other day, in the storm, I had been riding through a flooded street, and while heading to what I thought was a more shallow section, I had hit the flooded curb, and ended up tipped off Fiona, into the hidden flooded gutter. That's when, we think, the screen on my phone was smashed. Bother. But this shop can only fix the screen for €100, and it will take seven days. We ride away.

Initially, the climb wasn't too steep or arduous, and we thought that the tunnel might mean we had summited. But no. The climb, up to Volastra, was ugly. Steep, steep, steep, and narrow, but at least there was hardly any traffic. Ju did magnificently. I struggled. 100m at a time, but I cycled the whole thing. I know from experience, that Fiona is harder to push uphill, than cycle uphill. She's heavy. Then just before the top, a cyclist stopped and asked us whether we knew that the road was closed up ahead? What? What? Pardon? Our plan was to sleep in Corniglia, then return to the top road, and cycle further along the coast. Now the only option was to cycle over halfway up the hill, return to sea level, then cycle the same height again, to get past the road blockage. The downhill to Corniglia was amazing. The thought of having to cycle back up, twice, horrific.

We stayed in Corniglia two nights, delaying tactics and walked the trails to Vernazza. It was a stunning walk, with amazing views. This area of Italy is impressive. During the walk we decided that to cycle out of Corniglia was not going to be a fun option. Perhaps we could use the train, the 10km through to Levanto, because the climb out of there might not be quite as severe. Sounds like a very good option.

It's an adventure, translating the train timetable, buying and clipping the tickets, getting loaded bikes to the correct platform, and squeezing them on to the train, but we manage. Then we start the climb. 15km, and it's relentless, but not nearly as steep as our descent two days ago, so we're both pretty happy, although my legs are jelly by the time we reach the top. The reward: 15km of amazing flat riding, 600m above the valley, then 15km of whoopee downhill. YES. I love cycle touring. Every day has a challenge. Every day has highs and lows. Every day has its unknowns. And today was topped off, by my lovely lady telling me that today's ride was the best day so far of her trip in Italy. Gotta love that kind of feedback.

SUDDENLY CYCLE TOURERS

12th March 2016

Rapallo to Genova 51km
To Finale Ligure 72km
To San Remo 75km

The new cycle touring season must have begun. After several months of not meeting cycle tourers, in the last two days we have met four different groups, heading east. It's great to know we are not alone.

The adventures continue, but not all are on the road. Juliet and I decided to watch the sunset from the roof top terrace in Corniglia. No problem. It was stunning, if not a little breezy, so she didn't have her book and wine. The best of the sunset is done, and we are ready to return to our warm room, but the door to the roof has been closed and locked. There is no other way off the terrace. Damn. This happened to us in Las Vegas a few years ago. Some loud knocking on walls, doors and windows, and eventually a grumpy Italian opens the door for us. *"The Terrace is closed in the winter."*

We arrive in Genova. Juliet is keen to sort her train ticket back to Roma. That goes well, but it has been a tough day. A steady climb earlier on, a fantastic downhill, where I managed to zoom past a couple of road cyclists. They were not happy seeing a loaded touring bike and trailer passing them, and some tricky navigation, through heavy traffic, to find the railway station, so we were both pretty weary, after only 51km. But while Ju was sorting her ticket, I'd done some homework, and located some cheap hotels. Yep, they were in a very narrow, dark back street. Yep, there were heaps of Africans and Asians, and a few dodgy looking Italians hanging out, but these were prime one-star establishments, far superior to what I've been used to. I have to admit, I wasn't too comfortable. So, we moved one street over.

Ju checked a room out, in a hotel on the third floor. She was happy, so we loaded all the panniers into the lift. I carried two bikes and the trailer up the stairs to the hotel, but where is Juliet with all the bags? She's on the wrong floor. The hotel is on the third floor if you climb the stairs. It's on the second floor if you use the lift! Ju is lost. Sorry, not lost, just confused.

I've ridden 35,000km as of today, through over thirty countries. I'm a little more aggressive through traffic than Juliet, well not aggressive; I just seem to be able to pass through traffic easier than she does. It takes a while to tune in to traffic conditions. So, Ju is not always happy with my cycling style. I think she reckons I'm leaving her behind. But I would never do that. I'm very much enjoying having her with me. Her stay is just far too short.

We are camping on a small ledge above the sea, 30m from the road. There is no traffic noise, as the road passes through a tunnel. There have been several tunnels over the last couple of days. There have also been several sections of cycle trail. One really nice section was an old disused railway line, passing directly along the coast. It has been converted to a cycle and walking trail, with lots of tunnels and bridges, amazing views, and best of all, no traffic hassles. Every day in Italy, there are new experiences, and new adventures.

It's Saturday, so there are heaps of cyclists on the road, but today there seem to be even more than usual. We stop for a short break, and a policeman approaches us. He has seen my NZ Silver Fern and wants to talk about the All Blacks. He tells us that tomorrow, Sunday, there is a race for non-professionals. 3000 riders are expected. We are glad we will be off the road.

We meet yet another couple of cycle tourers heading east. They are from Spain, and heading to Australia, and perhaps NZ. They tell us of the great cycleway, 15km of it, through tunnels and along the coast all the way into San Remo. We find it, and it's fantastic, and busy with cyclists, walkers and skaters. And so, Juliet's cycling is over. We now have two days of rest and relaxation before she jumps on the train to Rome, and fly's home. Damn.

155 DAYS AND COUNTING

15th March 2016

San Remo

I guess we were pretty lucky to get a room in San Remo, but we are also very lucky to arrive the day before the annual Flower Show. 1000s had come to San Remo to see it and watch the Sunday morning parade of floats. I was not particularly interested in the flowers, but on Saturday night, we had seen a couple of jazzy 'marching bands' that were going to be in the parade, so I was keen to see them. Talk about packing them in. The streets were lined eight deep with oldies, mostly shorter than Ju and I, it's not often I feel tall. We stood, pressed boobs to bums, for half an hour, as the crowd swelled. Some very enthusiastic Medics were running up and down the street dealing with unwell members of the crowd, so they kept us amused. Finally, the parade came, but very few of the bands were actually playing as they passed us. Bother.

We spent Monday packing Ju's bike, and shopping. Ju looked. I watched the crowds. And then Tuesday morning she left...

The huge hills, wet, cold days, extreme heat, and hundreds of kilometers all seem so easy compared with how hard it was to say goodbye to my wonderful Juliet this morning. See you in Los Angeles my angel.

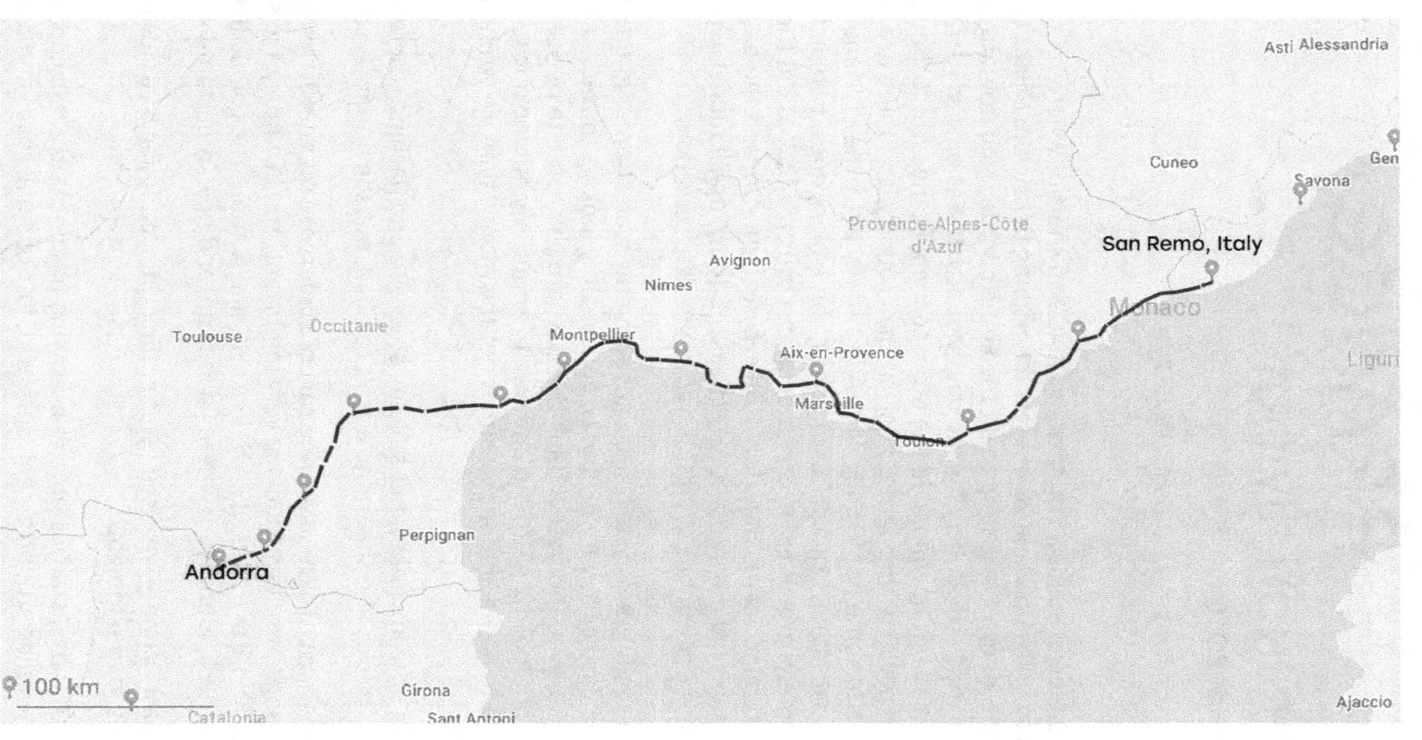

Asti Alessandria
Cuneo
Gen
Savona
Provence-Alpes-Côte d'Azur
San Remo, Italy
Avignon
Nimes
Monaco
Toulouse
Occitanie
Montpellier
Aix-en-Provence
Liguria
Marseille
Toulon
Perpignan
Andorra
100 km
Girona
Catalonia
Sant Antoni
Ajaccio

FRANCE

THE FRENCH RIVIERA

16th March 2016

San Remo to Mandelieu la Napoule 100km
To La Londe les Maures 101km

After a wonderful holiday, I'm now about 400km short of where I should be, so I need to make up some kilometers if I'm going to catch my flight to USA. So, I'm off. It doesn't take long to hit the French border, and not long after that, I'm in my third country for the day, Monaco. It was only as I arrived that I realised I had not downloaded the Monaco map. Bother. But it shouldn't be too hard to navigate through. It's only a small country, and there are signs. There are also some hot looking cars. A few of my petrol head friends would have been salivating. I saw some red ones, some black ones, two pink ones, and a gun metal grey Russian one that almost took me out, as did the big black Land Rover. Seems they don't like cyclists here. Oh, and the navigation? Following signs led me into a very unpleasant, fumy, uphill tunnel, which led me back into France, but at least it was in the right direction.

Nice had a really good cycle track, right along the waterfront, right across the city. Lots of flash cars, very big boats, and wealthy looking tourists, and the beach wasn't even too flash. I think this is where you come to be seen, and to flash your hot looking girlfriend and wealth about. My hot looking girlfriend is on a train to Rome, and my wealth is not the money type, so wrong kind of city for me.

Antibes is a little lower key, but still lots of wealth and flashing. There were some cycle tracks, and the traffic wasn't too bad, but still not my type of city.

Cannes was a zoo. There was some sort of conference on, maybe real estate, and thousands of suits, all looking very important, and in a hurry. I'm sure I was the only visitor in the city, not in a suit, and without the colourful lanyard around my neck, identifying where I was from, and how important I was.

Not long past Cannes, I realised I was getting tired, so found a campsite. No flash hotels for me tonight.

Heading out today, and yesterday's headwind has become a tailwind, mostly, except, I'm cycling around a peninsula, with lots of small coves and bays. I'm cycling slightly downhill, with the wind at my back, and not even pedalling, and I'm breaking the 30kph speed limit by 20kph. Then I turn a corner, and it's like hitting a wall. It's down to granny gear and 5kph. The wind is very strong and is ripping the surf up the beach and on to the rocks. It's spectacular, and these tiny bays are outstandingly beautiful. Some are totally protected from the wind and the water is calm. Others are exposed and are being thrashed by the waves. Juliet would have loved it.

It's exciting riding through the storm. Being pushed about by the wind, splashed by the surf, but around lunch time it starts to rain. I'm climbing up a scenic valley. There are heaps of great places to camp, but it's persisting down. After an hour or so, it's no longer exciting. I'm cold and getting tired. A cycle path takes me into a town, one I've never heard of, and I find a hotel. It's time to dry out. This is my sort if town.

TWITS ON BIKES

18th March 2016

La Londe les Maures to Resquiadou 120km
To Saints Maries de la Mer 112km

Juliet has arrived back in Christchurch, sans luggage. Some delightful rogue decided that he deserved to own her bike, and everything in her bike bag, and walked off the train with it, somewhere between San Remo and Rome. Ju was a little upset. She likes her stuff, and her bike has had many adventures with her. I hope all her stuff goes to a worthy home.

Meanwhile, I'm cycling into a beautiful small bay and hear a roar over my left shoulder. Wow that's a loud truck. I look back, and it's not a truck, its four very large aircraft, skimming above the surf towards me. I stop, expecting to have to duck, and they turn in formation out towards the open sea, dropping lower, so as they are actually in the water. They then lift off the surface, and about 30m above the bay, release the water they have collected. They circuit again four times. They are firefighting aircraft, practicing loading. Impressive.

Yesterday's ride was pretty nice. Even the climb up the last hill before Marseille was pleasant. A lot of the day was spent navigating cycle tracks. They're great. Keeps you away from the traffic and allows you to get the occasional look at the surroundings. That's what I was doing, taking photos when I heard a *"Yip!"* and a toot. Two cycle tourers, one from Newcastle on Tyne, and one from Tunisia. Great chatting, yet again, exchanging stories and tips.

And then, at the top of a hill, a bunch of classic cars. I took some more photos, just to show I care about the needs of my petrol head mates. Hope they enjoy them. What I had been looking for was a campsite. There were some nice ones about, but they all had 'No Camping' signs. So, I did the downhill into Marseille.

Marseille is not a cycle friendly town. It has cycle lanes, and also 'No Cycling' signs on the roads, but the cycle lanes are not friendly. They often have curbing instead of ramps at intersections, pedestrians and old ladies with Zimmer frames are all over them, sometimes they disappear completely, and cars and trucks will frequently zip across them in front of you. And everywhere is busy, very busy.

I was trying to navigate all this at rush hour. At one stage I was cycling along tram tracks, between trams. Other times it was necessary to go the wrong way down one-way streets. I did whatever was needed, to make progress in the right direction. Marseille is also very dirty, and rough, with lots of dodgy people about, but maybe that was because I was near the docks. I was being very wary as I navigated through, towards a commercial campsite, which was no longer there. Oh well, wild camping then, but a little further out of the city. I passed a small hotel, went through a tunnel, and took a small side road, and ended up back at the small hotel. Guess I'll stay here then.

Through the tunnel again this morning, but I'm confused. I'm trying to navigate across a huge wetland, which has bike tracks and canal tracks, but to get to them it looks as if I will have to cycle on a motorway. In every other country the motorway signage has been green, and normal roads blue. Here, it seems to be opposite. I think I've worked out a route. I follow some small roads along the coast for 3km, and suddenly there is a huge padlocked gate, just before the bridge over the canal I was going to cross. Bother. I backtrack, and find an i-site, and it's open. The lovely lady inside gave me directions. She told me that *"giving directions is probably not enough to base a marriage on, even though I was very handsome."*

The directions involved going on to very, very busy roads, through very ugly industrial and port areas, with very, very big, and very fast-moving trucks. I was not comfortable, and some of the factories were pumping out some very unpleasant smoke and smells. I was coughing, and my eyes were watering, but, then I entered a lovely small village, and got lost. More directions, this time from the Village Gardener because they always know best. This time I ended up on a very pleasant, quiet road, and then on a dyke that passed through the wetlands. That's where I ran into heaps of "Twitters", that's bird watchers, on bikes. I asked one British Twit what they were watching out for. *"Oh whatever."* I offered to put on some lippy, and pose, so he could take a photo of a *"kiwi bird, very rare in this part of the world"*. He was not impressed and called me a fruit. Oh well, can't please everyone.

In the supermarket tonight, I met three young French people, who are three days into a kayaking trip from France to Istanbul, taking nine months. Now that would be an adventure. Maybe next year...

LOU VILLAGE

20th March 2016

Saints Maries de la Mer to Sete 95km
To Valras Plage 74km

Today would have to be a big part of what this amazing journey is all about. The whole idea was to join together places I had been before, and would like to see again, with so many of the places I had never seen or visited. And here I am, in Valras Plage.

Thirty years ago, I resigned from my job, teaching physical education at Amuri Area School, and accepted a job with PGL Young Adventure, managing a Sailing and Wind Surfing Centre, here on the French Mediterranean coast. Lisa and Paul, my kids, were four and five, but that didn't stop us. Quite a few of our friends thought we were crazy, and most still think I'm crazy, but for all four of us, it was the start of an amazing adventure.

Over the course of the next five months we met some amazing people, and had some amazing, fun times. Thanks to all those PGL staff, for a fantastic experience. The experience I gained in France in 1986 has helped me so very much over the years.

I'm back in Valras Plage, just down the road from Lou Village, our base camp. It's still there but has changed as you might expect. Thirty years of progress and development. But it's amazing being here, and has been amazing cycling here, especially over the last couple of days, as I recognise names of towns and villages that we visited in 1986. We bought bicycles when we arrived, and I used the siesta time each afternoon to explore, perhaps my first taste of cycle touring. The small villages, with locals drinking wine and playing boules in the village square, haven't changed. The narrow streets and church bells ringing are the same. Today I was overrun by locals heading to church with branches (Olive?). I even spotted a couple of old Renault 4's, our site vehicle, way back then.

Way back then, I was also introduced to the canals and canal paths in the region and thought I might like to travel along them one day. I was thinking by long boat, but cycling them, over the last few days, have been pretty fun too.

And even though it's off-season here in the south of France, Valras Plage was pretty busy today, with families out for their Sunday wander. Oh, and the 100 plus members of the local Harley Davidson Chapter out for their Sunday ride. Noisy brutes, but impressive.

So, it's great to be back. Thanks, PGL, for the opportunity, the education, the learning, the memories, the inspiration to try new things in life, for the lifelong friendships, and the inspiration to come back for a look see. I've really enjoyed the memories.

THE SMALL VILLAGE OF EUROPE

21st March 2016

Valras Plage to Carcassonne 92km

Some of the trails next to the canals are wet and muddy, and are tough, slow going, so today I decided to go across country. I planned a route that would take me through some small villages, eighteen of them, and all in a straight line between my start and finish point, and except for the last 5km, on small rural roads. Living in a small village, 900 people, in New Zealand. I'm a small village type person. But you don't realise how isolated our village, Hanmer Springs, is compared with so many other countries. Here in southern France, as I exited one village, I would be able to see at least the church spire of the next, and often much more. They are very close together. But they are all unique.

Almost all have a large church, many have a mansion or chateau, most have a school, a couple of bars, a medical centre, and a bread shop. They all have narrow twisting streets that meant I got a little disorientated a few times, and all seem to have old ladies or men, taking up the whole width of the street with their Zimmer frame or walking sticks. But some are on the side of a hill or canal, some at crossroads or where canals meet, and some on top of a small hill. They all have some sort of central Piazza where the townsfolk meet for wine, coffee, a chat, and boules. Once you find this Piazza, it's hard to draw yourself away, and hard to find which is the correct route out. There is often, no obvious route.

What I can't figure out is the opening hours for shops and businesses. At no time, does it seem as if everything is open. Some seem to open at 9am, others at 10am. Most pull down the shutters at noon, and some reopen around 4pm. And in the small villages it seems that opening hours are even more random. In the tourist and holiday towns, I can understand the randomness, as it is off-season, but these small villages are not frequented by tourists. I guess you just have to live there to understand what is open when.

So, I had a fun day, and I got to chat to locals, who are always interested in my journey, and my trailer, and I also met a family from Spain, cycling to Sete, and three French lads, heading home from six months cycling in Spain and Portugal. The scenery was kind on the eyes as well. But the aim for the day was the walled Cité de Carcassonne. I had a small blonde or senior moment today, not that I qualify for either. I was sitting beside a canal, looking at the happenings at a complicated road junction. I noticed that all the streets were "Rue" this or that. My next thought was, "I wonder why they call all the streets French names." I decided it was time for a rest day. I've cycled over 700km since Juliet left, and I've got some big hills, the Pyrenees, looming. A bit of laundry, lots of food and sleep seems like a good idea to me. And where better to do that, than in a castle. I came here in 1986 with Lisa and Paul, aged four and five. I don't recognise anything from that visit, so I'm sure they won't remember much either, but it must have been exciting for them, visiting a 'real castle'. I'm excited to be here at sixty-one. And I'm resting, and eating, and my clothes are clean and I'm happy.

MAYBE THE MAYONAISSE

24th March 2016

Carcassonne to La Souco Negro 75km
To Hospitalet pres Andorra 54km

Oh wow, these medieval castles, with their high walls and narrow twisting streets, create quite a draft on windy days, and this morning the wind is bitterly cold and gets right up your kilt. I managed a kilometre, being buffeted from wall to wall, before I realised just how cold it was. Then it was on with additional layers, extra gloves, another hat, even longs. I wish I hadn't packed my extra socks so deep. But I suppose it was fitting, as today I was heading into the Pyrenees.

I had spent the previous evening talking English, to some native English speakers, which was a real treat. A family from Vancouver Island, BC, Canada, on a spring break holiday. Mum and Dad were surfers, now kite surfers, who in their youth had toured the world looking for the perfect wave. They must have found it in NZ, because they decided that they would emigrate there, but family ties at home mean they still live in Canada.

I navigated the very complicated one-way system out of Carcassonne, and then I began to climb. I could see shadows of mountains in the distance, in the haze, and I was excited to be heading there. But it was definitely up. Not since Armenia had I been so cold but sweating so much because of the climbing that was happening. Definitely granny gear stuff. Amazingly, even as I climbed, the villages were not far apart, so the odd local that was about was interested in *"what the heck are you doing, climbing this hill, and with a trailer?"* One old fellah on sticks, shuffled out of a cafe while I was having a breather. He had seen my NZ Fern flag. *"NZ? Rugby? All Blacks très bon. Daniel Carter fantastic."* It took me a while to understand the last bit. It was only the way the old fellah was acting out the flicking of the Rugby ball to the number 12, that I clicked and understood the French pronunciation of Daniel Carter.

The villages were very small, so it became obvious that I was going to need to camp out tonight. But I've climbed to 1200m, and the wind is strong and chilling. Luckily, just when I felt like my legs were about to give out, a small dirt road headed off to the left, into a copse of trees. Along this road I found a wonderful spot, protected from the wind. All night I could hear the roaring of the wind through the tops of the trees, it's just a little spooky.

Day two and I'm still climbing. There is very little traffic, except for the odd school bus. They are all heading to the top of the road, where there is a ski school. Not a lot of snow, but school was operating. It's at 1400m. And the views are amazing. I'm definitely in amongst some amazing mountains. And then the downhill began. For the first time ever, I'm not happy about downhill. It was glorious, sweeping bends, smooth roads, and no traffic, but I had just struggled up 1400m, and every metre down I would have to reclaim, as the highest pass into Andorra was about 2000m. Damn downhill.

700m we dropped into a pretty, sunny town, with a gondola heading up out of it to the ski fields on the southern side of the valley, it's time for food. The first restaurant I visited didn't serve food until noon, so I opted for a delicious filled roll, chicken, salad, mayonnaise. It was yummy, and then Fiona and I started climbing again.

The scenery is amazing, and the wind has dropped. I get to take off some layers of clothes. There is more traffic, as now I'm on the main road to Andorra. And the uphill is unrelenting. From Carcassonne to Andorra is about 170km. I figured three days of climbing, so at 50ish km, when my legs are screaming, "No more. STOP!", and a 'Camping' sign appears, it seems like an omen. The camping is actually closed, but there are no gates nor barriers, and really nice sites. I find one, protected from the wind, and with amazing views across the valley to beautiful, snow covered mountains, and sit in the sun and read my book.

When the sun drops behind the tops, the temperature plummets. I climb into my sleeping bag, even though it's only 6pm, and am asleep pretty quick. But I'm woken by cramps, and a bout of VnD 's. Not pleasant, and unexpected. Maybe the mayonnaise? The only bonus is, there is a full moon, and despite the freezing cold, I'm standing naked, staring at the beauty and glory of those mountains, standing so close, and so clear in the wonderful moonlight. It's great to be here.

ANDORRA

26th March 2016

Hospitalet pres Andorra to Andorra la Vella 48km

12km took me three hours. The views and scenery were spectacular, and almost made up for the screaming of my legs, almost. There was a good deal more traffic, most with skis or snowboards, and moving fast, as snow bunnies worldwide do, on their way to a day on the slopes. I was knackered, and after a night emptying my stomach and bowels, and not feeling like too much breakfast, my energy levels were not high. And then I turned a corner. Oh Wow. Suddenly, a big town, with ski lifts, and huge shops, and lots of ski runs. Not what I was expecting. It's Pass de la Casa.

There is still a climb of about 1km, and there is a tunnel option, but its Péage and 'NOT for Velo', so I push on. I need food. I cross an invisible line, and I'm no longer in France, but have entered the Principality of Andorra. The big shops are all open, selling tax free booze and cigarettes, but I can't find anywhere open to buy food. *"But Mr, it's Easter, Good Friday, and a holiday. Food shops don't open until the evening, except McDonald's"*. I had no idea it was Friday. I had no idea it was Good Friday. But I was so hungry. Chicken nuggets - disgusting, fries - I couldn't eat them, but the coke was hoovered. The body knows what it needs, and today it needed sugar.

Now there's another 5km of climb, but it's steady, and follows the edge of the ski field, so there's plenty to look at, and the skiing looks great. Perhaps I should jump on a snowboard for the rest of the day? Nope, my legs are already jellied. The climb reminds me very much of climbing with Tessa in NW India, but this time I didn't have her motivating me, and I was pretty certain I wouldn't see the utter chaos we found at the top in India. I'm about 500m from the top, and a road cyclist passes me. When I reach the summit, he is waiting for me. He congratulates me on my effort. He is a semi pro from Spain (Catalonia), spending the long weekend in the Pyrenees training. I'm pretty chuffed that he thinks I've done well. I'm pretty chuffed to be at the top; 2408m, after climbing to 1400m, and going down to 700m. Yep I'm feeling proud.

The downhill, oh goodness gracious me; awesome. There was almost 30km of it, and steep, and fast. Woohooo. There's a lot of skiing happening down the valley too. There are lots of people about. It's a boomer holiday weekend, and next week there is a World Cup Ski event here. I zoom past the downhill course. I need to stop to see where I am. A delightful man and his daughter offer me help and advice, without even being asked. I'm liking Andorra. They point out a camping site, and I head there. It's busy, it is Easter weekend, but there is space for a small tent. Yippee. And just below the campsite is the National Soccer stadium and I get to watch my first Soccer International, Serbia vs. Andorra, from the Scotsman's stands. Yep I like this country.

Except when I go to the toilet and I plug my battery pack in a socket to give it a boost while I'm in the cubicle. I come out, and it's gone. Damn. This is only the second time on my trip when I've had something stolen. The other was in India, my cycle light. I didn't expect it from a wealthy nation.

A family from Catalonia, hear I've had my charger stolen, and find a spare, which they give to me, and a little later turn up with a bottle of wine, which would normally go straight to my lovely Juliet. I had to turn it down. It's a little while since I've been treated so nicely by the local population. Sorry Italy and France.

On a wander this evening, I find the shops open. Everything. But it's Good Friday? I buy a new battery pack, and get my glasses tightened, and I walk past a brand-new Rugby Stadium. A team is training. I stop to watch. It's Latvia, and tomorrow they play Andorra. I'm chatting to the injured Andorran winger. He tells me I should come and watch. It will only cost about €5.00. I think I might.

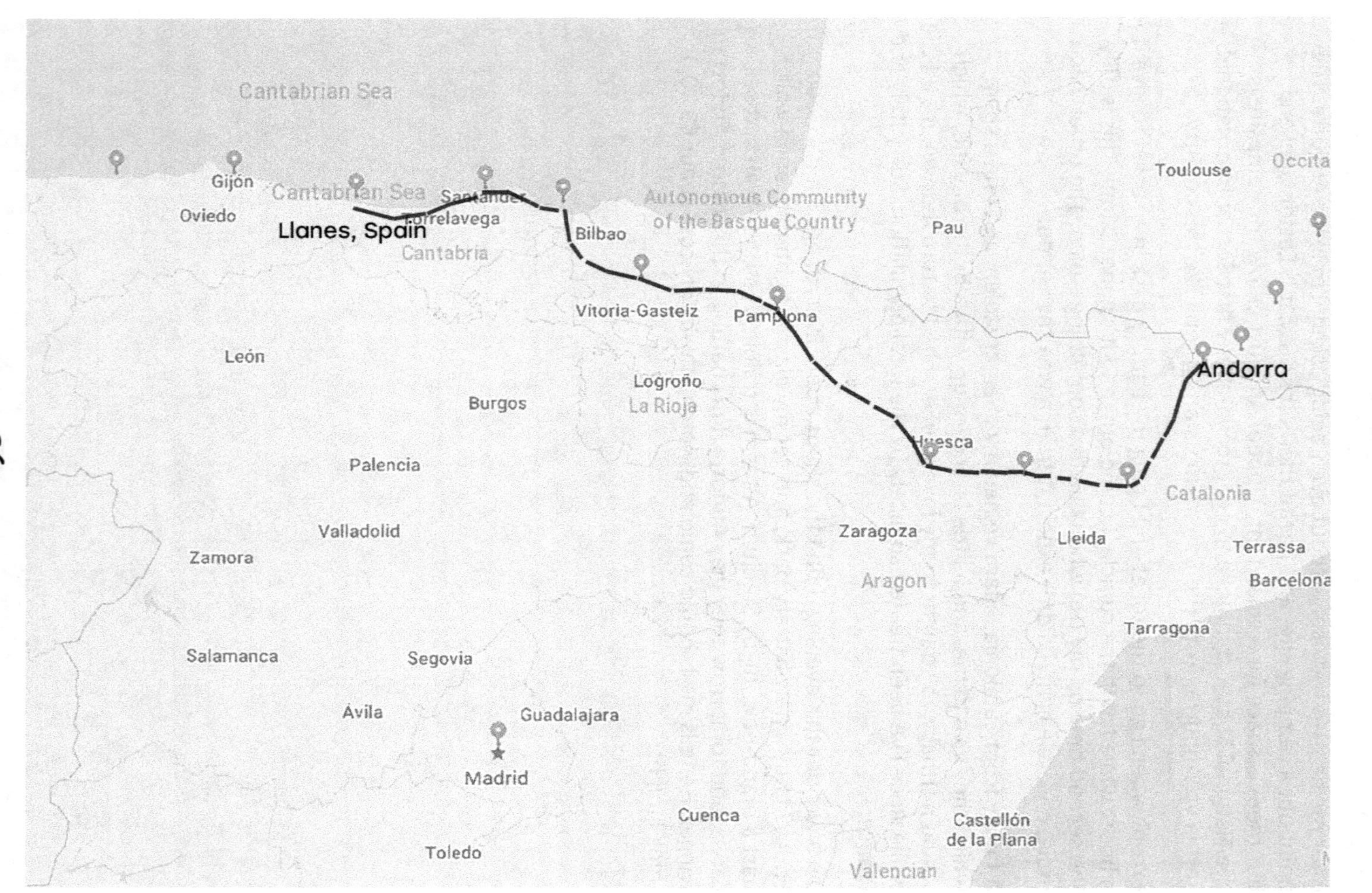

Cantabrian Sea
Gijón
Cantabrian Sea
Santander
Oviedo
Torrelavega
Llanes, Spain
Bilbao
Cantabria
Autonomous Community
of the Basque Country
Pau
Toulouse
Occita
Vitoria-Gasteiz
Pamplona
Andorra
León
Logroño
La Rioja
Burgos
Huesca
Catalonia
Palencia
Zaragoza
Lleida
Terrassa
Valladolid
Aragon
Barcelona
Zamora
Tarragona
Salamanca
Segovia
Ávila
Guadalajara
Madrid
Cuenca
Castellón
de la Plana
Toledo
Valencian

SPAIN

RANDOM ADVENTURES

28th March 2016

Andorra la Vella to Cubells 107km
To Monzon 76km

I love the random stuff you run into on a cycling adventure. Over the weekend I got to see two International sporting events: Andorra playing Serbia at soccer and Andorra playing Latvia at rugby. I've got to say, that the rugby was a lot more interesting and fun. The crowd at the Rugby was loud and funny, and three times bigger than the soccer crowd, 600 versus 200. The soccer had ten policemen on the grounds, with two police dogs. The rugby had zero police. Andorra got beaten in both games. At one stage, the Andorran rugby team, which seemed very young, had only nine men standing. Bodies littered the field. And it cost nothing to watch; incredible. An international event with no entry fee. Wow.

The other random event over the weekend was the Andorra Sax Festival. I only saw the bands marching/dancing in the streets; small bands, of about ten or twelve, trumpets, trombones, saxophones, tubas and percussion, with the odd guitar thrown in. What great entertainment. The Festival lasted a week, and included workshops, performances and competitions, as well as the street marching. Everyone was having a lot of fun, and what fantastic atmosphere.

I dragged myself away from Andorra, and swept into Catalonia, a soon to be independent state? It was Easter Sunday, and I had stocked up on food for the day, realising that not much would be open; but oh boy. I didn't realise that Spain has even more stringent Easter trading laws than NZ. Nothing was open on Sunday or Monday, except the odd hotel/restaurant, that you had to be staying at to get fed, and petrol stations. I ran out of food. The hotels were very busy, dining rooms crowded, and with long queues, and they were only serving toasted sandwiches. I stopped at a petrol station, and only reluctantly, while no one was watching, would the attendant sell me a coke and a packet of lollies. He was only allowed to sell petrol. And I had eaten all the food I had; all of it.

But then I ran into something else, a road cone. About a dozen guys were working at the edge of the road. They were very busy, and dressed in bright yellow, with a big yellow truck, so easy to see. I was watching them, as they were dodging about randomly, and didn't see the road cone. It tossed me across the road, and I was surprised I didn't eat tarseal, but managed to stay upright. Fiona wasn't as lucky. The front tyre came out of the rim, and the wheel was pretty badly buckled. Damn. I played with the spokes and straightened it enough to ride, but it needs work. 15km to the next town.

With lots of help I am directed to a bike shop. It's not open, because it's Easter Monday, but peering into the dark, I notice the shop is empty. A motorist stops and tells me the shop has moved to the next town, another 10km.

I can't find the shop. Lots of people confirm its here, but it's well hidden. I find a hotel, and sneak in a feed five minutes before the kitchen closes, but it was yummy, or was I just very hungry. I meet a lovely Spanish (Catalonian) couple who have spent Easter mountain climbing. I think they're going to come and visit us in NZ.

Random things you 'run' into make an adventure.

WHEAT, WIND & SWINE

29th March 2016

On a farm, you call a bunch of cattle a herd, and a bunch of sheep a flock. On a wind farm, do you have a 'zephyr' of windmills? What about a solar farm, perhaps an 'aray' of solar panels? There are certainly numerous wind farms in this part of Spain, and I've seen two enormous acreages of solar panels. Tell me again. Why are we not doing much of this type of farming in NZ? Do we not have enough wind or sunshine? And why is it so expensive to install solar panels on your house? Seems several third and second world countries manage.

As well as power, they farm wheat and pigs, and the pigs, housed in long houses, stink. When you think you've finally got upwind, you pass farmers spraying pig effluent on the wheat fields. It's hard to get away from the smell. I camped about a kilometre from one long house. The wind changed overnight, and I had a headache in the morning. I could also hear the pigs squealing all night. Not a pleasant way to farm.

I had left Monzon at lunchtime, having shouted Fiona a new front wheel. The guy at Dr Bike had straightened the buckle, but when he tried to 'true' it, the wheel 'tacoed', bent in half. He was not prepared to guarantee that it wouldn't happen again, *"perhaps tomorrow, perhaps in a month"*. I was happy to buy a new wheel. This was the same rim that had been damaged when I hit a dog in Tajikistan, so I was pretty happy at how long it had lasted, as the mechanic in Dushanbe had been a little worried about how much strength the rim still had. 13,000km since then, so that's not bad kilometres.

I wanted to make up some kilometres, and had planned a cross country route, on tiny rural roads, through quiet villages. Spain seems bigger than Italy and France. The distances between villages is greater, but the only traffic on the roads was tractors with spraying gear, and trucks, transporting pigs or grain, from silo to pig sties. I was hearing what I thought was woodpeckers, but where were the trees. There were only pylons, and tall church steeples, and ancient, European silos. I looked up: Storks, building nests. What amazingly huge birds, to be building nests in such exposed precarious sites? The woodpecker noise was the storks clucking. Occasionally there were also large birds of prey circulating in the thermals above my head, which gives you some incentive to not find yourself splattered on the road.

Finally, I'm starting to recognise some of the language. I thought I wouldn't have too many problems. Italian, French and Spanish words seem to be scattered throughout the English language, but since arriving in Andorra, I've had no clue. But I now know why. They were all speaking Catalonian. For the last two days, I've been hearing real Spanish, but everyone I speak to expects me to speak Spanish, and they rattle on speedily, while I look on blankly. Now I'm in Basque Country, another independent state? and they speak Basque. I'm still in the dark, and back to using sign language.

I had a bit of a lively tailwind yesterday and managed my largest kilometers of the adventure, so far: 179km, woohooo, which gives me time for a wander around Pamplona today. These streets would be crazy scary in July, being chased by bulls.

BAY OF BISCAY

4th April 2016

Pamplona to La Corta Lake 96km
To Castro Udallies 103km
To Santander 64km
To Llanes 95km

Every day, I'm still challenged. The last few days have been cold, wet and windy. I seem to be going uphill about 75% of the time (Spain is hilly). My knees are sore, and I've bruised my tailbone, so the only thing I can sit on in comfort, is my bike seat. And while all this is happening, you notice different stuff. I bet you've never noticed that motorways seem to go flat and straight. On the 'passage for bicylettes', I seem to be often looking down on the motorway, as it screams across the valley, and then punches through a tunnel beneath the mountain, or up at it, as it flies across the inlet, river or gorge, on 30m high concrete supports, while I skirt around the bay, up the valley to a tiny bridge, and begin the climb over the ridge.

Another thing that's bugging me is that Spain has changed its clocks to European Summertime, and NZ has changed from Daylight Saving time, and I can't work out what the time difference is between them. And as a result, I'm finding it hard to chat to Juliet, when one of us is not meant to be sleeping, or she's not driving around in an ambulance, or flying around in helicopters. Grrrr.

And then the opening hours of Spanish shops. It's doing my head in. Saturday and Sunday are the worst. The only way I know its weekend, is that there are so many more groups of cyclists out on the road. Then I realise I haven't got enough food and am nowhere near a shop or supermarket. When I finish cycling for the day, normally about 4pm, I'm hungry. But nothing is open, except a few bars, but they don't sell food, only cocktails. Restaurant kitchens open at about 8pm, way too late for my grumbling tummy, and supermarkets open around six thirty, maybe, but not on Sunday, and often, not on Saturday. Breakfast is served in some hotels, hostels, and bars/cafes, but it's all croissants and sweet chocolate pastries, not really the energy food I need before six or seven hours cycling. Grrrr

But at least I'm not walking. I'm meeting heaps of people, from all over the world, Japan, Korea, USA, Brazil, Germany, France, Spain, walking the 800km of the Camino de Santiago, an ancient Pilgrims route across Europe to the shrine of St someone. Apparently, there are several routes, I'm following the coastal northern route, and thousands walk it every year. The only sensible group I've met, are a group from Southern Spain, who are mountain biking the northern route. I've tried a couple of sections, which were pretty nice, but three times I've ended up on very rough rocky, muddy or sandy trails, so aren't bothering any more, just following the roads that run parallel. Yikes, there are some crazies. Who'd walk 800km with a heavy pack?

But there has been a highlight this week. I've reached the Bay of Biscay, which is really the Atlantic Ocean. Woohooo. I can't believe it. I've cycled west from Hanmer Springs to the Atlantic Ocean. I'm pretty chuffed with that, and there are some beautiful bays and seaside villages to pass through and climb out of.

THE RAIN IN SPAIN

7th April 2016

Llanes to Gijon 98km
To Luarca 102km
To Foz 75km

Contrary to what Professor Higgins thinks, the rain in Spain falls mainly on
Grum, whether he's in the mountains, on the coast, or on the plains. I've had
two days lately, where I've been totally drenched, and also a couple of days of
horrendous winds. I was crossing a couple of causeways and was truly afraid
for my welfare. I was leaning into the wind, but when a vehicle passed, the
absence of the wind would almost toss me off the side of the road. So, I took
a couple of shortcuts - ferry's across some tidal inlets. One was very short,
about five minutes, but the other was about twenty minutes, and just a little
rough. All was good, until the skipper turned towards the wharf. Then Fiona
did a slide, and I thought she was going to go swimming, fully loaded. But she
hung on in, and I scraped her off the deck, and hauled her ashore. It gave me
a bit of a heart flutter though.

But all is not bad. I took a friends advice and found some happy pills in aisle
14 beside the frozen goods. The sun came out to play, and things always
seem easier in the sunshine. I've been meeting a few 'pilgrims' walking the
Camino. They're finding it a bit hard. Some steep sections up and down
to beaches, and some tough asphalt stretches. Nope. I'm happy to be on
my bike. Yesterday, for almost 30km, I followed along parallel to the coast,
around a ridge, then down some lovely declines to a bridge, before climbing
again. The downhills were fun, the uphill not too steep, I often passed under
the motorway twice on each loop, and it all happened in a lovely eucalyptus
forest. Felt and smelt, just like cycling in Aussie. I was just waiting for the
famous drop bear to appear, when I went round a bend, and met an Aussie
couple from Byron Bay way. It was great being able to chat to someone that
you can almost understand.

My roommate the other night, we were the only two in a 200-bed hostel, was
a Korean American. She had trained as a Doctor, but never registered, instead
has been practicing Eastern medicine. Talking to her was very interesting,
and I asked heaps of questions. She told me she regards the human body as
its own universe. Four limbs (four seasons), five vital organs (five oceans),
six other organs (six continents), and much more, that I missed, as I was
counting. She also talked about diet, and how the percentage of types of

teeth should correspond with the percentage of types of food you eat. For example, four canine teeth mean 16% of your diet should be meat, while 64% of your teeth being for crushing grains. The numbers astounded and confused me, but totally fascinating thinking. She also showed me some exercise that will help combat Prostate, and Breast Cancers. Interesting.

Then I meet a young French nurse, and a young German mechanical engineer. Both were dissatisfied with their jobs, so quit them, and came to find themselves, walking the Camino Santiago. I congratulated them, as one piece of advice I give, to those who bother to listen, is, "If you're not happy, quit, and move on." It was nice to meet some youngsters doing exactly that.

The road code here in Spain insists vehicles give at least 1.5m of space to a cyclist, and almost all do so. On windy roads, they will slow right down to my speed, until they are certain they can pass legally and safely. It's so nice to be respected.

My shoe squeaks. For a few weeks now, I've had what I thought was a squeaky front wheel. Before I hit the road cone, I had a slight wobble in the front wheel, but I couldn't find why I had a squeak. Then the wheel was changed, and no squeak, until it rained, and the squeak returned. I searched but couldn't find the source. I rode around a car park in my socks. No squeak. I put on my shoes. A squeak. Damn, I'm glad it's not the new wheel.

The gardeners in all the small villages are busy, mowing lawns, weed-eating road edges, all in preparation for the Most Beautiful Village on the Coast competition. It doesn't feel many months ago that I was cycling past farmers, using a hand scythe to cut similar length growth, but scraping all the cuttings into a basket, and carrying it all 5km back to their one cattle beast for feed. It is amazing the different values various societies have.

Today I'm in Foz. (Love the name) It's a small coastal village, with a great cliff top walk. The sea was a tempest today, with huge waves and incredible shoreline action. The weather and nature create some amazing spectacles.

37,000km done today. The question is: do I continue to follow the coastline, or cut across country to Santiago de Compostela with the Pilgrims?

CAMINO DE SANTIAGO

11th April 2016

Foz to Ortigueria 78km
To Betanzos 80km
To Santiago de Compostela 54km

The good news is, as I cycle out of Betanzos, I spot a sign after about a kilometre, that tells me it's only 57km to Santiago, not the 74km we had calculated. The bad news is the "drizzle" predicted, is already torrential rain, and I'm already slogging uphill. And both the uphill and downpour continue for the next twenty kilometres. After that, the wind hits me. I've been wet on this adventure before. I've also been cold before, but this is the first time I've been both wet, to the skin, and cold, freezing. I duck into a bus shelter and put on more clothes, not that it offers much shelter, and then as I take off again, it hails. Damn. I thought it was meant to be getting warmer. It's spring for goodness sake. There's nowhere to stop for shelter, everything is closed because it's Sunday. My body takes over, setting a mechanical rhythm, and my mind turns off, focusing only on staying safe on the road, rather than thinking about how frigging cold it is, and how much I'm hurting; and then a sign tells me 10km to go. Woohoo. I can do this.

Last night I had stayed in a sixty-bed hostel, with one other guy, a Canadian writer, living in Spain. Normally he writes about food and wine, but right now he's researching two books on the Camino de Santiago. He walked here fifteen years ago, and this season he is walking all the routes, about nine different trails, some of them twice. He reckons he will have walked 2400km by the end of summer. That's some feat.

We got talking about the empty hostels. He told me the summer is really busy. They are expecting over 250,000 Pilgrims in 2016. Then he explained the math. A private hostel might have thirty beds. Every bed earns €15.00 a night for five months, and then if they choose to feed those pilgrims that's another €10.00, and laundry, €5.00. A family make a substantial living over the busy five months, and the routes are so popular, the season is extending.

He told me that between May and August, there are not enough beds on the routes. So, some pilgrims will get up at 4am, waking everyone else with their rustling and head torches, and then virtually run to the next accommodation, so as to grab a bed. The government is offering all sorts of incentives to locals to renovate old buildings into hostels.

Another business that is doing very well is transporting of luggage along the route, so the hikers don't have to carry full packs. However, this is really annoying those who choose to carry full loads, as when they arrive at hostels, the 'light loaders' have nabbed all the beds. Riots are predicted.

When you start your pilgrimage, you buy, for €1.50, a passport. Everywhere you stop, you get a stamp, hostels, pubs, restaurants, info centres. When you present this passport to the Pilgrims Office in Santiago, you get a certificate, showing how far you walked. I got the passport, and the stamps, but haven't bothered with the certificate. I got the passport, because with it you also can get discounts, for food and bed nights.

So, its big business and a lot of people are walking a long way, between 200km and 800km. I've been watching them arrive. Some heavily laden others with day packs. What they have in common is that many are hurting by the time they get here, injuries, sore feet, aching backs, and they all seem to be in a hurry. My Canadian mate reckons almost all don't give themselves enough time to complete the Camino at leisure. They book a flight before they leave, and then have to push hard to get here in time to catch the flight. The other thing I observed as the Pilgrims arrive is, they walk into the main square loaded with their pack. They stand and stare at the cathedral. They turn 360° and look around the square, and then they look at each other as if to say, "Well we've done it. What now?" I'm told that the month of walking is life changing, and many come back and do another route. I guess some of them actually do the walk for the religious significance of it all

I pushed on through the rain, because I wanted to have a rest day on my birthday. Today I'm sixty-two. I've celebrated by visiting a barber, eating cake, and sleeping. I'm pretty sure I might even have a second rest day tomorrow. It's still persisting.

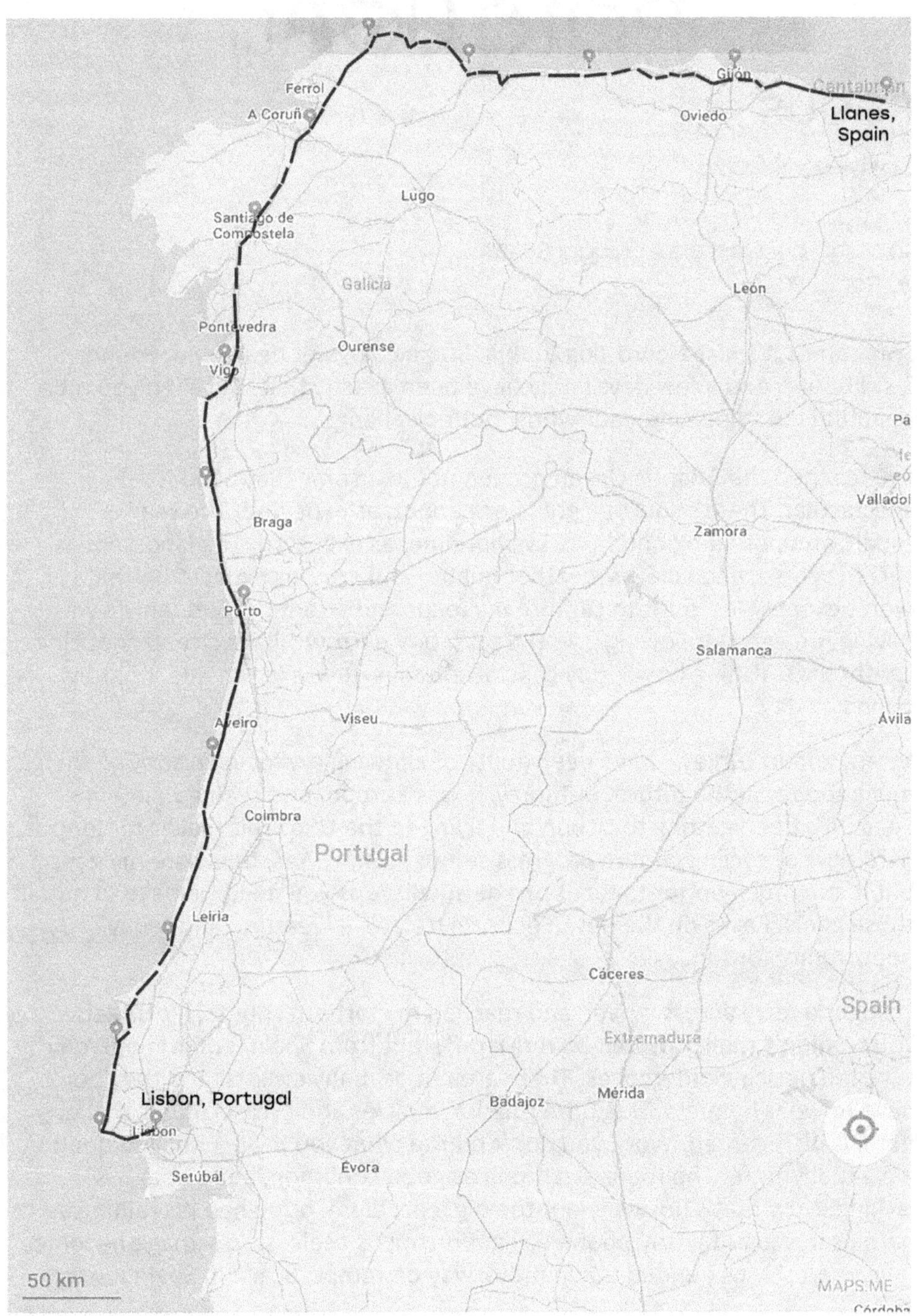

Llanes, Spain
Ferrol
A Coruña
Oviedo
Gijón
Cantabria
Lugo
Santiago de Compostela
León
Galicia
Pontevedra
Ourense
Vigo
Valladolid
Braga
Zamora
Porto
Salamanca
Aveiro
Viseu
Ávila
Coimbra
Portugal
Leiria
Cáceres
Spain
Extremadura
Lisbon, Portugal
Mérida
Badajoz
Lisbon
Setúbal
Évora
Córdoba
50 km
MAPS.ME

PORTUGAL

FOCUS

16th April 2016

Santiago to Vigo 97km
To Viano dol Castelo Portugal 84km
To Porto 80km

Sometimes it's just a hard slog, uphill, into a cold, wet headwind. Sounds just like life. And a few days lately have been exactly that. But then you hit a beautiful coastline, and your whole outlook changes.

I've reached the Atlantic Ocean proper, not just some 'Bay', and it's spectacular. There's sort of a grey haze about, as expected. The sea is rough, and pounding onto a rocky shoreline, as expected. The landscape is sort of sparse, and villages weather beaten and grey, as expected. What I didn't expect was, for it to capture my focus and attention. Suddenly, I was having fun again, following gravel tracks, tiny narrow village streets, noticing lighthouses, fishing boats, tiny coastal cottages. It was great, and it hardly rained all day.

Lately, and in Turkey, I have been guilty of allowing my focus to stray to things much too far in the future. In Turkey, it was Europe, and seeing Juliet. In Spain, it's been getting to Lisbon and flying to the USA. This makes for long hard days of cycling, where progress seems so slow. Yes, those are my goals, but it's so much better to focus on the small steps you need to make to obtain those goals. Focus on the now. Focus on today's adventure, and today's opportunity for fun.

I caught a ferry across a river, and reached my fortieth country, Portugal. You wouldn't think it would be much different from Spain, but immediately I started noticing differences. There are not as many cyclists, and they don't have to wear helmets. The 1.5m rule for vehicles and cyclists, if it is a rule here, is disregarded. Wow, you don't realise what you have, until you don't have it anymore. The roads are not in as good condition, and signage is lacking. Now that's normally not too big a problem, but when it's raining as hard as it was today, my phone navigation app is useless, so signage becomes important. Twice I ended up on motorway on ramps. Scary. In Spain it was also possible to do this, with just a few seconds inattention, but a sign usually grabbed your focus. Not so in Portugal. At one stage I ended up on a very busy dual carriageway for 5km, which was not pleasant.

But I made it safely to Porto. Wow. This is a big city, over three million souls, and tons of history. I don't think it has ever really registered to me before, but for a lot of people it is the centre of their life. That's what I'm finding so fascinating about this amazing adventure; learning every day. I'm going to stay two nights and do a free walking tour.

(If anyone is contemplating walking the Camino Santiago, I would recommend the Coastal Route from Lisbon. It's stunning, and very quiet.)

PORTO

17th April 2016

The city where Port Wine comes from.

The city that fought a war against its own country and won.

The city with world famous bridges.

The city where J K Rowling lived and apparently got lots of inspiration for *Harry Potter*.

The city where the Mayor encourages Street Art.

The city that has a ghost in its railway station.

Who knew??? All new learning for me, thanks to free walking tours, and the YES Hostel.

SUNNY SUNDAY

19th April 2016

Porto to Praia de Mira 101km
To Nazarè 120km
To Santa Cruz 98km

Every man, his wife, his family, and her dog, was at the beach. But oh the dogs… I apologise already if I offend but European women and their dogs. Ladies! Dogs have legs and can walk and run. They don't need to be carried. They also have fur, hair or wool. They don't need clothes. And please, train your dog's not to yap, yap, yap at cyclists. Three rat-like animals came through a cat flap, shoulder to shoulder. I think they were dogs, they yapped, but they were dressed in so many layers of clothing, I couldn't tell, and they were exhausted after chasing me for 10m. I was scared to put my foot down, in case I squashed them.

So, the beaches, or should I say the car parks above the beaches were crowded. Hardly anyone was on the sand, and the only people in the sea were a couple of body boarders. They all got out of the city, because it was a sunny Sunday. I had problems though. I had a route planned, around the coast, but the road was closed. I had to climb over a ridge, but that hooked up with a very complicated dual carriageway heading to one of the bridges. I ended up in the hospital grounds, so skipped along some footpaths, around some one way corners, the wrong way, down a short muddy track, and down a very narrow cobbled street, with a couple of steps, down a very quiet, traffic free valley, and finally hit the coast road again. Yeeha.

I've got to say, cycling in sunshine is a lot more pleasant than in rain. All day I stayed off major roads, finding obscure back lanes, passing through eucalyptus forest, farmland, cabbage patches, and olive trees. It was fun. As I rode through yet another cobbled main street of a small village, I realised how lucky I am. So many of my friends would love to be doing this, and here I am. "Ho hum, another pretty little village, Ho hum". Then I realised that I've only got a couple more days of these amazing European villages, and then I will be cycling through the 'new world' villages of the USA. That's why I decided to climb up to my last European castle. It was very steep, and it hurt, and I sneaked in through the castle wall through a gate that said, 'No Entry', onto really ugly, bouncy cobbles. I bounced through a few streets, dodging tourists. There were 100s of them. The village was amazing. Dodging the tourists and bouncing along the cobbles wasn't. I headed out again, through the main gates, past a knight in armour, a medieval doctor in a mask, and a wizard with a huge sword, and the ticket booth where there was a queue of tourists waiting to pay to get into the village, and twenty something buses.

The Mountain bike Orienteering World Champs are in Portugal in July. I reckon I stumbled upon the competition area, kilometre after kilometre of beautiful tracked forest. If it wasn't the area, it should be. And through the area, covered in well-spaced conifer and eucalyptus, was a very quiet road, with an amazing unused cycle track. What an incredible day, of wonderful traffic free, scenery watching, sunny and warm cycling. This Atlantic Coast is turning out to be some of the most enjoyable cycling of this whole trip.

I've noticed another difference between Portugal and Spain. In Spain, and France, and Italy, every supermarket had a beggar standing outside the door. In Italy, this was often an African, who offers to carry your groceries. In France and Spain, it was usually a European. In Portugal, so far, no beggar outside supermarkets.

All these countries do have traffic lights just before small villages. They show as red, and as you approach, if you're not breaking the speed limit, the change to flashing amber. However, here in Portugal, they don't register Fiona and I, so stay red. We do what most the locals do. Ignore the lights and keep on going.

I was on a ferry, crossing an inlet, and a local cyclist came over to chat. I love these times. He offered to show me a route through the next town. He also asked to borrow my pump. The pump worked really well, but every time we screwed it off, it took the valve out as well, and the tyre ended up dead flat. Damn. Eventually, we solved the problem, two of us holding various parts of the pump, tyre and valve. I'm not sure the tyre was all that firm in the end though. He offered to buy me a meal. Lovely locals.

Yesterday, after 120km, I'm looking for somewhere to stay. I come to a roundabout. To the left, and uphill, is a campsite. To the right, and downhill, is sign-posted Bombeiros. Bombeiros are medic/fire-fighters. The two services are combined. I had heard from other cyclists that sometimes they will let you stay at their base. Yippee. I've been invited to sleep over; hot showers, kitchen, games room, TV room, lounge and bar, and at least thirty beds, and at no cost. However, the night crew all decided to sleep in the same room as me, and although they had zero call outs, all five of them snored like troopers.

CYCLE ACROSS ASIA AND EUROPE. TICK

20th April 2016

Cabo da Roca Portugal

Today Fiona and I stood together on the western most point of Europe; forty Countries, 37,945km, 698 days, and I'm feeling very proud of our achievement.

LISBON

24th April 2016

Santa Cruz to Lisbon 109km

Probably the most stunning coastline I have ridden along in the almost two years of this journey. That's how I would sum up Portugal's Atlantic Coast. With amazing beaches, bays, villages, views, and surf, along with beautiful cycle lanes through stunning forest, on quiet, traffic free roads. A cyclist's dream route.

I had no idea there was even such a thing as a World Surfing Reserve, but obviously a few others did. Some spectacular surf breaks, and a few hardy souls out enjoying them. It looked a bit chilly to me, but I'm not a surfer, but also looked spectacular, and threatened to lessen my kilometres for the day, as I was suckered into standing on roadside vantage points, watching the surfers having fun. Seven reserves/breaks along the coast make up the park, and I'm sure they must be pretty busy at times. Today it was pleasant and relaxing, to watch.

A British voice asked, *"Did you really cycle all the way from NZ?"* "Yep." *"Wow. This is my partner, she's from Auckland."* It turns out the young lady in question is from Thames, via Devonport, now living in Southampton, and they are on a surfing holiday. It's really nice to chat to a kiwi.

The highlight of the week however, was reaching the western most point of Europe. I celebrated by eating chocolate, taking photos, and reflecting. Yes, this is a significant milestone.

Then there were 30km of coastal highway into Lisbon, through a couple of very pretty beach towns, and there are people swimming and sunbathing. It is significantly warmer. I had planned to follow bike trails into the city, but the traffic was light, and the road smooth and wide, so didn't bother. The cobblestones in the city however were not so smooth, and the first three hostels I visited were full. Bother.

The Sunset Destination Hostel has to be one of the best I've stayed at, with lovely staff, great breakfasts, and a rooftop bar and pool, overlooking the river. I'm glad I found it, as waiting in Lisbon for five days before catching a train to Madrid, and flight to New York, seems like a long time. I fill my time with a couple of free walking tours. On one I meet two young kiwi ladies, living in London, and on another I meet a Lithuanian Concert pianist, tutoring here in Lisbon for a semester. She is an amazingly talented lady, inspirational when it comes to her music, and a great guide. She introduced me to some interesting parts of the city, and some yummy Portuguese pastries.

And then I attended the Anzac service hosted by the Australian Embassy, a small but poignant ceremony, at the Lisbon War Memorial. The service was further away than I realised, so I was running late. I decided to jog. Fitness was no problem, but oh my, the thighs were being used in a totally different way from cycling. By the time I arrived, just after the Aussie national anthem, they were burning. This time last year, Ju and I had been at the Australian Embassy in Kathmandu, for the ceremony, followed soon after by the Nepali earthquakes, not something I wanted to repeat this year.

There are a lot of tourists in Lisbon. It must be crazy in the summer. I'm not a fan of pushing through crowds to see ruined buildings, ancient churches, famous shops and restaurants. Instead, I've spent my time sitting by the pool, reading my book, with the occasional cooling dip, a welcome respite before the excitement of visiting my final country on this adventure. The USA.

SPAIN

MADRID

29th April 2016

To be honest, I was a little stressed about the train trip to Madrid. Even though I had my ticket, and the ticket seller assured me I could take Fiona into my compartment, I've heard stories of cyclists not being allowed to board with their bikes. It only takes one overzealous official to ruin a good day, but today, I had nice guys. I squeezed Fiona and the trailer into the compartment and climbed onto the bed and slept all night. The reason it was so comfortable was we were stopped somewhere for four hours. We arrived in Madrid at noon instead of 8am.

I cycled to a hostel, but they had nowhere secure for Fiona, so I started dismantling her straight away, which went well, except a few of the rack bolts, the pedals, and the seat post, which haven't been touched for almost two years, were solidly stuck. Never mind, there's a cycle shop nearby. I hoist skeletal, sans wheels, Fiona onto my shoulder and wander the streets of Madrid looking for it, getting some funny looks. Of course, it's Siesta. They open again in 30mins, at 5pm, and then; soooo helpful. The seized bolts are dealt with, and then I'm given the 'Royal Tour' of the oldest bike shop in Madrid's museum, pretty damn amazing. This is a manufacturing bike shop - Otero - and I'm shown ancient bikes, drawings, photos, tons of medals and cups, and the bike that won a gold medal at Barcelona Olympics, and the 1992 Olympic Torch. And I was given a medal, *"because anyone who has cycled from NZ to the Atlantic deserves a medal"*. I'm humbled. Thank you so much Otero team.

Then it's back to packing. I've been trying for months to book some extra baggage on the flight to New York, but I can't do it online. I'm worried about that, and also about my weight allowance. I'm only allowed one 23kg bag. Flying from Delhi to Bishkek, I had a 60kg allowance. I shuffle and change stuff from bike bag to trailer, then carry them to a Pharmacy to weigh them: 22.5kg in bike bag, 27kg in trailer. I go back to my room and shuffle some more and throw some stuff out. I'm stressed again and spend two sleepless nights trying to devise cunning schemes to get everything on the flight.

By mid-afternoon I give up. I hook up with another free walking tour. This guide was good, enthusiastic, interesting, funny, and entertaining. If you're in Madrid I recommend him, or one of his colleagues, outside the i-site in Mayor Square, wearing a red shirt, with a red umbrella. His girlfriend was a bit all right too. I learnt about the Moors, the Jews, the Christians, the royal families, the Inquisition, and the Incest; interesting.

Musicians are everywhere in Madrid; violins, accordions, guitars, and even crystal glasses being played. There were also lots of characters to have your photo taken with, including Puss in Boots, Minions, and a rotund Spiderman, who was actually pretty funny. There were also lots of African salesmen. They lay out a sheet with their wares, soccer shirts, or shoes, or leather bags, or sunglasses, but they never let go of the 'tie ropes'. It's fun to watch them. They are very alert to the police. Spot one, and within seconds, they have pulled their 'tie ropes', the wares become a large white bundle draped over their shoulder, and they disappear up a side street. The police pass by, and the salesmen are back, laying out their sheets. In twenty minutes, I saw them pack up and leave five times. The cleverest things I saw on the streets were the living statues. These guys are made up to look like statues, and hold poses for ages. One guy was dressed as a soldier and was holding a pose as if he was running on attack. I don't know how he held it for so long. It must have been incredibly uncomfortable.

My flight leaves at 11.15am. I get a taxi just before 7am. What an amazing surprise at the check in counter. No hassle, zero, nil, nada. Trailer 23kg. Bike bag 23.5kg. I wrap the trailer, which has the two bike carriers tied to it, in security wrapper. I pay €60.00, and both of my luggage articles are whisked away to the plane. Luckily, I'm early, as the flight is leaving at 10.15am. That could have been an Oooops. Less than eight hours later, I'm in the USA. Woohoo. I've been looking forward to this for a very long time.

USA

NEW YORK TO SAN FRANCISCO

7,600KM 100 DAYS

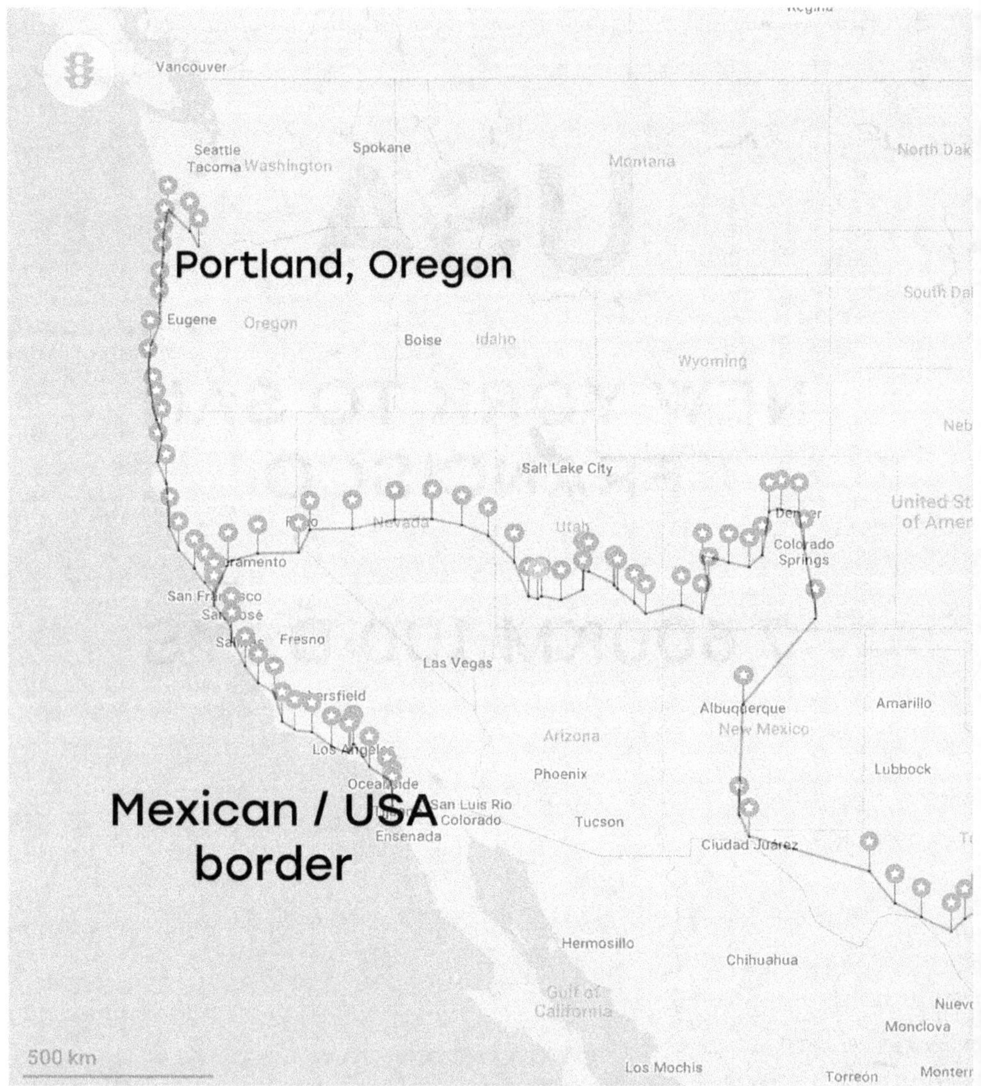

Vancouver
Seattle
Tacoma
Washington
Spokane
Montana
North Dak
Portland, Oregon
Eugene
Oregon
Boise
Idaho
Wyoming
South Dak
Neb
Salt Lake City
Reno
Nevada
Utah
Denver
Colorado
Springs
United St
of Amer
Sacramento
San Francisco
San José
Salinas
Fresno
Las Vegas
Bakersfield
Albuquerque
New Mexico
Amarillo
Los Angeles
Arizona
Lubbock
Oceanside
Phoenix
San Luis Rio
Colorado
Tucson
Mexican / USA
border
Ensenada
Ciudad Juárez
Hermosillo
Chihuahua
Nuevo
Monclova
Gulf of
California
500 km
Los Mochis
Torreón
Monterr

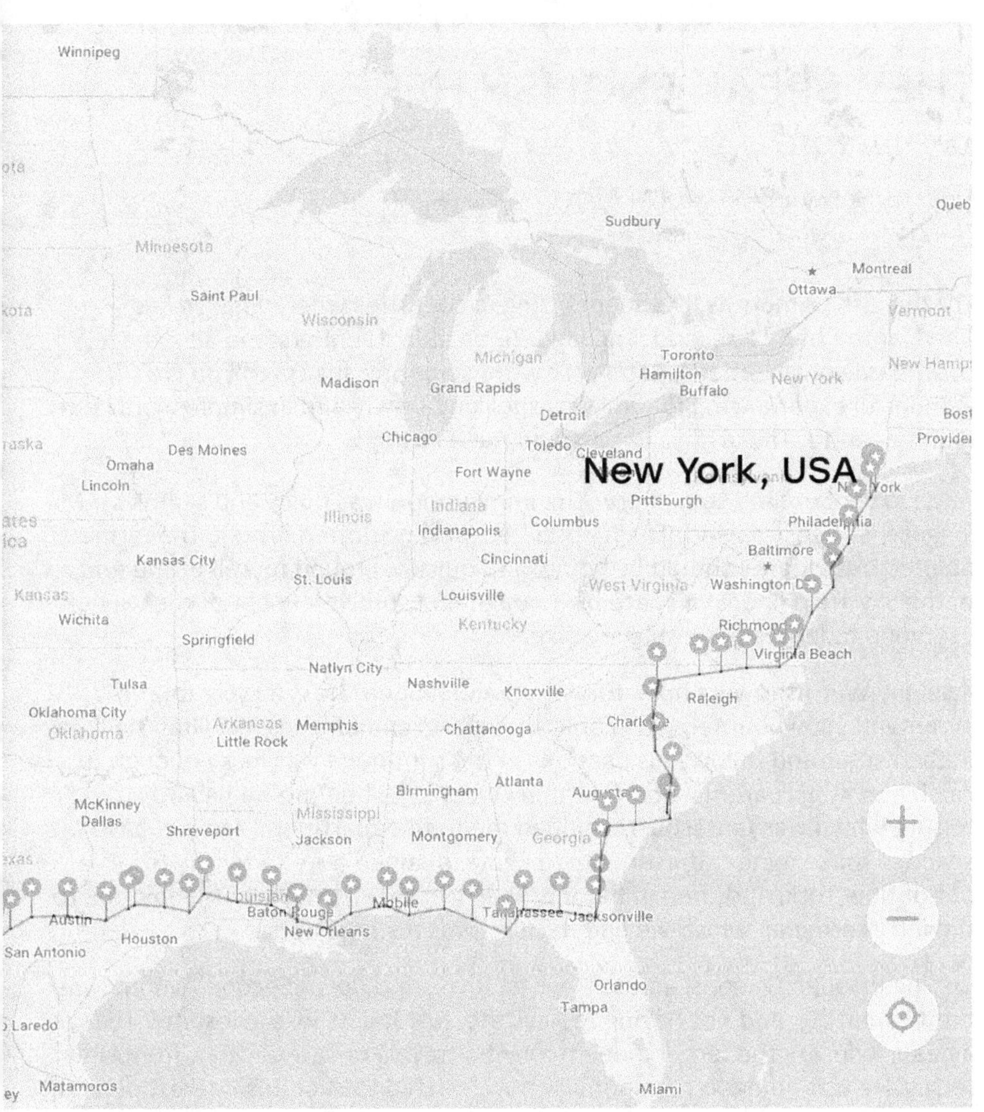

Winnipeg
Quebec
Minnesota
Sudbury
Saint Paul
Montreal
Ottawa
Wisconsin
Vermont
Michigan
Toronto
Hamilton
New York
New Hamp
Madison
Grand Rapids
Buffalo
Detroit
Chicago
Toledo
Cleveland
Bost
Des Moines
Fort Wayne
New York, USA
Provide
Omaha
Pittsburgh
New York
Lincoln
Indiana
Illinois
Columbus
Philadelphia
Indianapolis
Cincinnati
Baltimore
Kansas City
St. Louis
West Virginia
Washington D
Louisville
Richmond
Kansas
Kentucky
Wichita
Virginia Beach
Springfield
Natlyn City
Nashville
Raleigh
Tulsa
Knoxville
Oklahoma City
Charlotte
Oklahoma
Arkansas
Memphis
Chattanooga
Little Rock
Atlanta
Birmingham
Augusta
McKinney
Dallas
Mississippi
Shreveport
Jackson
Montgomery
Georgia
Texas
Louisiana
Austin
Baton Rouge
Mobile
Tallahassee
Jacksonville
Houston
New Orleans
San Antonio
Orlando
Laredo
Tampa
Matamoros
Miami

UNITED STATES OF AMERICA

THEY SPEAK ENGLISH HERE

1st May 2016

Queens/New York/USA to Whiting New Jersey 97km
To Egg Harbour Township 80km

For the last 18 months I've been cycling in countries where English has been, at the best, a second language. To be able to understand all signage, overheard conversations, and every word someone speaks to you is a wonderful experience. I found I was speaking slowly and in simple words but didn't need to. These guys understand me. Exciting!

And I'm very excited to be here. The immigration was quick and seamless. My luggage was easy to find. The helpful 'red jackets' dotted around the terminal pointed out where I should be going, and quickly, I found myself at the end of the Sky Train line, in a space big enough and sufficiently out of the way of everyone to let me assemble my bike.

Kyle, my Warmshowers host, turned up and helped. He is a cycle tourer, surfer and snowboarder, who cooks breakfasts and lunches in a Utah ski area in the winter and follows his passions in the summer. I was lucky enough to catch him at his parents' apartment in Queens, just before he flew to Hawai'i to surf, which was fantastic. He guided me to the apartment, fed me, gave me space to make minor adjustments to Fiona, planned a route for me to cycle out of New York, and then in the morning, cycled with me into Manhattan, to the ferry terminal, which we had decided was my best option.

Cycling through Queens, across the East River, and down Second Avenue was pretty amazing, and not having to navigate, just follow was awesome. Thanks a heap, Kyle. On the ferry I met a man who travels on it every day, from New Jersey. He was going to nap, but when we started to chat, his interest perked him up. *"You're cycling to LA? Like LA, Los Angeles? In California? You've cycled from NZ? Around the world from NZ? Excuse me while I text my girlfriend and tell her."* He points out landmarks, Ellis Island and the Statue of Liberty. He takes phone calls and tells his friends about me. As we leave the ferry, and everyone stares at Fiona, he tells them, *"He's cycling to LA. He's cycled from NZ."* He tells me he is my new biggest fan. Funny.

I'm hungry. I spot 'The Girls Diner'. $5.00 buys me a breakfast burrito and an orange juice. Yummy. I think I'm going to put on weight. I'm cycling a bicycle-friendly boardwalk. There are lots of people about. It's a warm, sunny Saturday, and there are preparations happening for a 1st of May Marathon. I stopped for an ice-cream, so many flavours. I stop at a supermarket, so much choice. And I understand all the signage and am familiar with so much of the food. I'm so very much excited to be here. My face is aching from grinning all day.

I find a campsite, 50m from a very quiet road, in pine trees, on a bed of pine needles. The last few nights my sleep has been broken. Noisy hostels, bumpy trains, stress about excess luggage, and my body reminding me about jet lag. Tonight, I sleep thirteen hours, uninterrupted. I wake to rain, eat breakfast in the tent, and pack everything up, before quickly squashing a very wet tent into a dry bag. The road is very quiet, good advice Kyle. I see hawks, eagles, Canadian geese, turkeys and lots of birds that I think might be jays. I'm almost taken out by a couple of deer that bound across the road in front of me. I'm soaking wet, and cold, but smiling. I stop at another diner. The Eagles are playing on the radio, followed by Neil Diamond. 'Vote for Donald Trump' stickers are plastered everywhere. I'm in America. Omelette, toast, home fries, two hot chocolates and free internet, all for $5.00, and no complaints about the puddle I left on the floor. I love this.

My next Warmshowers hosts are heading away tomorrow in their 'trailer' on vacation. Some of the family, including grandchildren are here. What a wonderful atmosphere to step into. Yep. I'm having fun.

THE ATLANTIC COAST CAPES

4th May 2016

Egg Harbour Township to Lewis 78km
To Ocean City Maryland 65km
To Tasley Virginia 125km

Oh my, they have a few rules here. I thought I was in the Land of the Free.
I pulled into the parking area to board a ferry, just as the last vehicle was
boarding. *"Hi sir. Have you a ticket?"* "No." *"You'll all have to get one from the
ticket office."* "Okay." *"Hello sir. You need to show me photo ID to get a ticket."*
Back in the car park. *"Now sir, we just need this dog to check you all out."*
My panniers, trailer, handlebar bag and pockets are sniffed. *"What are you
looking for?"* *"Just for anything you all shouldn't have."* said the Trooper. I'm
told that they are just checking this stranger out, as he's doing unusual stuff,
and they need to profile me, and get me in the system. Hmmmm.

Then the signage. 'NO Camping.' 'NO Swearing.' 'NO Skateboards.' 'NO...', and
they're everywhere. Is there anything you're allowed to do? And there are
soooo many churches, many of never before heard of denominations; 'The
Church of the Lighthouse to God', 'The Church of the Enlightened Father.'
Many are tucked away in quiet, tiny villages, and some are almost hidden in
the woods. Is this the Bible Belt?

But I'm meeting some amazing people, and can have in depth conversations
with them, using words longer than one syllable. Like Debbie, an intelligent,
beautiful pianist and organist, who teaches piano, is a massage therapist,
and has just sold her Mexican Restaurant, where she did all the cooking. I
considered a proposal, and an offer of coming to live with me in Hanmer
Springs, but she might not like that I'm already married, (and perhaps I need
to check in with Ju about it as well).

Then there's Alex. He's a beach lifeguard in the summer, cleans and prepares
swimming pools in the spring, and cycles to warmer climates in the winter,
so he can practice his passion of body boarding. This young man has his
priorities sorted.

What about the crew at the Tasley Firehouse? I can't find my Warmshowers
host, so call in to the Firehouse (Fire Station). The Chief is there, even though
he's a volunteer, and there isn't a call out. *"No problem, sir."* I love how polite
they are. *"You can bunk down here. I will just text the crew and let them know
you will be here. Do you want food?"* Over the course of the evening 'I guess'

every volunteer turned up to say, *"Howdy sir"*, and then they hung out. Some are taking a firefighting course at the academy, and had a written exam today, so there's a lot to talk about. Now I'm not sure whether they were really talking English, because when they got going, it was very hard to understand, but maybe that was because of the giant gobs of chewing tobacco they had stashed behind their lower lips, and their spitting into the empty bottle they have in the front pouch of their hoodie. I'm so very lucky, to be able to share these real American experiences. One of the crew was a policeman from the Chesapeake Tunnel/Bridge, and will help me cross it, since you're not allowed to cycle. Another couple suggested the best place locally for breakfast.

Ocean City has a huge boardwalk, and this weekend is Spring Festival, which looks very much like an A&P (Agricultural and Pastoral) show, but without the animals. Lots of marquees were being set up for stalls, and all sorts of rides to add to those already on the boardwalk. As I rode into Ocean City, I passed at least ten mini golf courses. But then it is usual for 350,000 people to descend on the area over the summer, which starts on Memorial Weekend, in three weeks. So, a pleasant quiet spot must turn a little crazy. What I did find, after much searching since arriving in NY, was an AT&T shop, and sorted a sim card for my phone, with the help of a great bunch of very respectful, and helpful staff. Did I say how much I love these people's manners, calling me "Sir".

And the scenery? My Warmshowers hosts have been recommending the best cycling routes. Mostly the routes stay well off the main roads. Yesterday I meandered through lovely forest roads, with very little traffic. I saw deer, heaps of bird life, including a huge flock of what I think were chicken hawks, and lots of other 'critters'. I just wish it would stop raining on me.

PLUS TAX

7th May 2016

Tasley Virginia to Chesapeake 112km
To Merchants Millpond SP 93km
To Roanoke Rapids 106km

It keeps happening. I've just eaten pancakes with maple syrup, and home fries ($5.35), and a hot chocolate ($2.00), and am ready to pay, $7.35 in hand. But no. The 'check' is $8.34. I've forgotten about tax, and let's not forget 15% to 20% tip. Yet again, a cheap breakfast costs over $10.00. Damn dumb foreigner. I'm south of the Mason Dixon Line (Google it, because it's significant), and I'm staying. If I was from the 'North' I'd be referred to as a 'damn Yankee'. I'm in Southern USA, and "Things are different down here boy." I cycle through a very small town, at a quiet road junction. There's a garage, and a general store, and on the veranda of the store are four old fellahs 'chawing down', watching the world go by, chewing tobacco, and spitting into a spittoon. Honestly. I would have taken a photo, but I'm not sure they would have appreciated the phone in their faces.

Last night I slept in a swamp, in bear country. There is signage everywhere telling me how to react if I'm confronted. 'Don't play dead.' I won't. Fiona will be flying.

I met a Southern Deputy Sheriff. I couldn't find my Warmshowers host. No answer on his phones, and no response to messages. Ah ha, a Sheriff's office. Maybe they can help.

"Don't know anyone by that name boy."

"Are they in gaol?"

"Why do you want them?"

"Even if I did, I wouldn't tell you where they live."

"No, I will not phone them, even if your phone is not working."

"No hotels in this area boy. You have to leave now; this office is closing."

"Yep I know it's getting dark, that's why I'm going home."

"Git boy, I got stuff to do."

Thank goodness for the camaraderie and support of the Fire and EMT community. A couple of nights later, I was hosted by a lovely couple, and he was a Sheriff's Deputy. He was horrified by my experience.

The Fire and EMT crew send me to a breakfast spot about 5 miles (8km) down the road. The chef greets me. *"Gidday mate. You must be that kiwi, kicking around on his bicycle."* His daughter visits NZ regularly. Loves NZers and the good weed. He is a *Lord of the Rings* fan and can't wait to visit, to try the weed.

There are so many run-down homes in this area. Ramshackle clapboard houses, trailer homes, and relocatable house's, and then suddenly, a row of southern mansions. All are lived in. There are few garages. Every building has half a dozen vehicles sitting around it, from the newest, cleanest (detailed) present ride, probably a big 'pickup', to rusty old derelicts that have sat unused for twenty years. I'm cycling through the history of American automobiles.

I'm also cycling through some amazing countryside, green, clean and refreshing. It's spring. There's lots of growth and lots of new life. I see turtles in the swamps, sitting on logs. When I stop to take photos, they quickly slip into the water. I've seen ground hogs, whistling frogs, possums, beaver, squirrels, loads of deer, and heaps of birds of prey, huge birds, with amazing wing spans, that have no fear of a lone cyclist. I'm feeling really close to nature, as many of the roads are really quiet, so I get right up close to the wildlife. Fantastic.

I'm hearing lots of opinions and getting them without any prodding. It seems a lone cyclist is someone people can speak to freely, sounding out their views without consequence:

Donald Trump is going to make America great again. (They really believe this)

I've no longer got any faith in politicians. They've ruined America for the ordinary person, while lining their own pockets.

I no longer have respect for the military and veterans. Why is America spending so much money, fighting and killing people overseas? They're no threat to us, and meanwhile, people here in the USA are poor and suffering.

No one in America is poor. They've all got a pickup and an iPad. They're not poor. - I've signed up to join the Marines. I want to be a full-time firefighter, but hopefully can get the training in the Marines, or afterwards through the GI Bill.

Who would vote for Trump, a multi-millionaire who has made his money out of the poor people working with rich Corporates? Do people really think he has had a change of heart, and as President, will work for the good of the people? I don't think so.

There is so much going on here; almost too much to take in. Perhaps it's because, for the first time in a long time, I can understand most of what is being said around me. My mind is whirling but I'm soaking it all in. I thought I knew the USA, but I'm learning, every day. Every day there is a WOW.

SHOTS FIRED

10th May 2016

It's Mother's Day. The supermarkets and florists are doing a roaring trade, flowers and 'Love you Mom' balloons seem to be the gifts of the day. The churches are all really busy as well. I've already talked about how many there are, sometimes in small villages, there is a different one on each corner of the main crossroads. You have to wonder where the entire congregation come from. What is also apparent is that almost all the churches are segregated, with black or white congregations. I'm told you can tell the difference, because the white folks' car park will be empty by noon, whereas the black worshippers stay on until it's done, and then they have a meal.

I've stopped outside a church, having a break. A car pulls into the car park next to me labelled: 'Visiting Pastor'. A tall, well-over-six-feet black dude climbs out. He is wearing a bright pink, sparkly shirt, and a large chain with a heavy silver cross around his neck. His purple suit fits his height but is about four times two wide for his slim build. He is wearing a wide brimmed purple felt hat. He is a pimp, a drug pusher, or a pastor. He comes over to me.

"Hello there Bossman. My name is Pastor Samuel J Claxton. Where y'all coming from?"

"New Zealand? My Lord. Gracious me. You'll come from NZ on your bicycle? You da Man. Gracious me."

"Where you'll going Bossman?"

"Los Angeles, California? Gracious me. Is that even possible? Dang. You really da Man. Oh, gracious me; may the Lord make you safe. Dang."

This could only be the USA. He then went inside to preach to his parishioners. I know he spoke about meeting me.

I must really focus on what these people are saying, otherwise I cannot understand their English. Standing behind two black guys in a supermarket queue, and I could not fathom what they were talking about. One fire-fighter introduced himself to me as "Gre". I asked him three times and was no wiser. His mate translated, "Garry". Usually, when talking to me, they slow down, and with a lot of concentration on my part, I gather the gist of the conversation. When they talk between themselves, I've got no idea. I may as well be back in Central Asia.

Three hours into a head wind and I've had it for the day. I pull into a town and spot a Fire/EMT Base. I'm in Henderson, and yep, I can pitch my tent, or claim a bed in the crew room. I choose the tent site. Not long after, "Curly" (bald) and "Slug" (like a bullet he says, like a snail his mates say), invite me to a barbecue dinner, hamburgers and hotdogs.

They want to know why I'm here in Henderson. "No tourists come here. Don't you know that we have the highest homicide rate in the state, the most shootings per capita, and more heroin overdoses than any of the surrounding four states? Why would you come here?"

I explain about my journey, about following my nose, meeting people, learning. I tell them I'm from New Zealand and started cycling from there two years ago.

Faces turn blank. "Where the heck is New Zealand?"

I get out my map, show them where NZ is and my route so far.

Jaws drop. They are astounded. Suddenly I'm a visitor of importance, not just some crazy old man on a bike. And when they hear I've been a volunteer firefighter and an EMT they totally open up. I'm a member of the family.

The whole crew — three fire fighters on one appliance, and six EMTs on three ambulances, plus a few volunteers manning various Rescue Vehicles — are on a twenty-four-hour watch. Wives and families join us for the BBQ, it is Mother's Day. It's a wonderful atmosphere. We all share food, talk about jobs, family, hunting (Slug is a keen turkey hunter), and so much more. I'm in my happy place, but it's QUIET. (You never say that word when you're working Emergency Services) The guys are getting fidgety. The Sheriff has delivered some confiscated illegal fireworks to the station, for the Fire Service to dispose of. "Let's light some." "Woohoo".

We return to the squad room. The large TV screen on the wall records all 911 calls, so the team can be prepared for call outs. The latest 911 call? 'Shots Fired. Beckett Street'. Damn, that's us. The Sheriff turns up. The Chief says, "Yep we all heard some noise. Not sure whether they were shots. Not sure where they came from. Might have been fireworks. Might happen again. It is Mother's Day." Sheriff leaves. "Let's fire off all the rest. Woohoo". For the second time tonight, the TV screen notes 'Shots Fired. Beckett Street'. Just another normal day in Henderson, North Carolina. Love it.

COUSINS, CAMPING & CIGARETTES

16th May 2016

Winston Salem.

I've spent the last few days in Winston Salem, with my cousins. Staying with family is amazing. The last time I did anything like that was in Kathmandu, at the 'Hanmer Springs Consulate'. With family, you can stretch out on the couch, sleep late, eat lots, and then eat again, argue and debate politics, foreign policies, religion and other touchy topics, and bait the young folk with outrageous arguments. And when you leave, they're just glad that their obnoxious cousin has finally left, and no harm is done to New Zealand's international reputation.

My cousins were wonderful. I'd been telling them for thirty years that I was coming to visit, but I don't think they ever expected that I would arrive from Hanmer Springs, New Zealand, on my bicycle. And I arrived at an auspicious time, as cousin Matthew and wife Jessica were being capped. Now that was an experience. Three days of ceremonies, gatherings, celebrations, and eating. I managed all the eating, but I reneged on the Day 3 ceremonies. Two days of sitting in chapels, listening to speeches and prayers, and watching columns of young people being 'hooded' (capped), was enough for me. But I did get to meet some really interesting people and see some big places.

Interestingly, Winston (a cigarette brand) Salem (another cigarette brand), is in the heart of tobacco growing country. Wake Forest University, which appears to be associated with the church, is situated in what was once part of a huge tobacco company. The whole area grew rich on tobacco. But now, the church, Baptist I think, has taken over. My cousin's church is huge. It has two gymnasiums, maybe a pool, and a huge sports area. It's also got a school, and has a congregation of 2000, a couple of choirs, at least one orchestra, and more than three different Sunday services, not counting several ethnic services. And just down the road is another church just as big. (Religion is BIG here). It just seems a little weird that cigarette and tobacco money has morphed into Baptist education. But it seems that it works, as something like 1500 students graduated this weekend, from medical, law and divinity schools, amongst others.

I also got to spend time with and know more about my cousins. Hannah, who is partway through her undergraduate degree, is studying for a medical school entrance exam that she must sit in the middle of her summer holidays. She fits her study into her busy schedule, which includes playing and lots of practice on the violin, and time at The Barn. The Barn is a riding school, and Hannah spends a couple of hours a day there with Ernie, her horse. She expects to 'show' him several times over the summer. How she fits it all in is amazing. She certainly has no time to get into trouble.

The others are just as busy, studying, working, and being incredibly talented musicians. Fitting in three days of celebrating graduations, and on top of that, making themselves available to entertain their obnoxious cousin from New Zealand hardly ruffled a feather. They helped me order new cycling sandals, get Fiona to a bike shop for a tune up, and advised me on routes out of town.

I met Tiffany, related by marriage. Wow, this young lady can cook. The very best blueberry muffins I've ever eaten, a scrumptious chicken pie, and chocolate chip pound cake. I'm sure I've put on a kilogram in weight. Rumour has it that near the new International Equestrian Centre in NW North Carolina, there will soon be a new restaurant, 'Lunch at Tiffany's'. I highly recommend you visit. You heard it first here.

Thank you, Faye and Tim., I had a wonderful time. I was rested, educated, challenged, overfed, hugged, and I felt the love only a family can give. I really enjoyed my time with y'all. Your home and family were always going to be a very significant 'dot' on my journey. See y'all again soon.

HEROES

20th May 2016

Winston Salem to Locust 127km
To Bethune SC 119km
To Kingstree 116km
To James Island 135km

Before I left Winston Salem, I prepared all my warm weather, dry gear. I changed the lenses in my cycling glasses to the darkest shade. I was expecting to be moving into warm, dry sunny areas. Instead, I left in heaving rain, and have been wet every day since.

The rain is not conducive to comfortable camping, and as I'm cycling a little-travelled route, along very quiet, narrow country roads, there are very few Warmshowers hosts. I have needed to resort to Option III. Almost every town has a Fire/Ambulance base, and the volunteers and permanent staff have been incredibly welcoming. Mostly I am given the run of the station. Often, I am offered beds, always food, a shower, and best of all, company. I'm pretty much over long nights alone in my tent.

At some stage during the evening, I get to tell my story. Initially it is received with a little disbelief, or lack of understanding. That's when I bring out my progress map, and show them where I've slept for the last 720 nights, where I started, how many countries I've passed through, and where I'm expecting to go before heading back to NZ. Suddenly, I'm raised upon a pedestal, somewhere I'm not comfortable standing, and phones and texts start flying, families and off duty members start turning up. My visit seems to have quite a bit of 'Wow' factor. I try to bring my exalted status back closer to normal by explaining that "I'm just an ordinary, but slightly crazy, old man, with an exceptionally understanding wife, who is attempting to cycle an average of 35 miles (60km) a day, for two and a half years." I also tell them that in reality, they are the heroes. They're the ones who drop everything at the beep of a pager—wife, kids, work, meals, sleep—and head out into the unknown, because someone they don't even know is in distress or danger.

But the best part is when the excitement settles, and I get to chat to these ordinary Americans.

One guy explained to me why he wears a sidearm whenever he leaves his house. *"There are bad guys out there. They might confront me at any time.*

Should my wife and children be with me, I need to be able to protect them. If either my wife or children were injured in any way, because I didn't have my firearm with me, I would not be able to forgive myself."

Another guy knows NZ only as the place where Bert Munro comes from. He has a 'motorsickle' and has watched *The Fastest Indian* five times. He doesn't ride his bike much these days, as "it's not too family friendly." A young fellah knows NZ because some of his heroes come from there. Works out this fellah and I have heroes in common, Sir Ed Hillary, Rob Hall and Mark Inglis. His dream is to visit Mt Everest. He almost cries when I show him photos from our cycle trip to Tibet's Base Camp.

I meet a nineteen-year-old female. She is very proud that she has almost paid off her mortgage for her own house and has almost finished refurbishing it. She has all sorts of plans for further study, new businesses, and travel.

I also met a retired US Navy officer, who had been seriously injured by an exploding mine. Then he became a Forestry Commission fire-fighter and fought fires all over the south of the USA. Now he is the grandfather/mentor to a whole new generation of young fire-fighters and EMT's. His passion is collecting shoulder patches from Fire and EMT units. He has none from outside the USA. How about we change that? I know many fire-fighters and EMT's.

Another young lady, she looks about seventeen, tells me she has a three-year-old, and is pregnant again, but her passion is being a member of the local volunteer fire brigade. She turns up to every call out, and practice and tonight is helping redecorate the new fire station.

The wife of one of the permanent staff, he is a fire-fighter and EMT, is excited to meet me, and hear my story. She asks me to visit her kid's school tomorrow. Okay. The visit is a treat, about forty eleven to thirteen-year olds. We have a great time. I tell my story, and they ask intelligent questions. Young Johnny is in the front row. *"If y'all going to Florida, my granmammy lives there. Sh'all put y'all up and feed y'all. And I've got ants in Georgia. Just tell them "Butter" sent y'all, and y'all be welcome. They all know me there."*

I met the Chiefs son. He is six years old. He whipped me at volleyball, soccer and tic tac toe. I asked him whether he was going to be a fire-fighter when he grew up. *"Nope. I'm going to be an EMT, a policeman, a fireman and a soldier."*

Last night I was invited to play cards with the duty crew. Somehow, they managed to not have any callouts until I had won the game and gone to bed. Then they spent most the rest of the night out being heroes.

TWO YEARS

25th May 2016

James Island to Charleston 37km
To Coosawhatchie 126km
To Statesboro Georgia 106km
To Madray Springs 108km

Two years ago, today, I cycled out of Hanmer Springs, with a bunch of friends. There were tears. I was off on my big adventure. Wow.

Two years today, my youngest grandson was born. Happy birthday Sebastian. Not long now until we meet in person. Wow.

Two years, forty-one countries, 25,000 miles (39,701km), and I'm still being wowed by what I'm seeing, and the people I'm meeting. Let me introduce some I've met this week.

Nicky is a full-time fire-fighter and EMT. She 'womans' a station in South Carolina with one other person. They have an ambulance, a fire appliance and a tanker. Depending on the type of call, they respond in two different vehicles. Sometimes Nicky 'womans' the station alone. She hopes others, from other stations, will turn up to assist her. Wow.

Nicky works hard at keeping fit, running and in the gym. However, she lives in Savannah Georgia, and there has been a spate of women joggers being grabbed off the street, so Nicky carries a firearm in a special pouch sewn into her running shorts. She also has a special holster sewn into her tank top. When she goes out socialising, she wears her gun under her skirt. She tells me that many of the church goers on Sunday will be wearing a gun. Wow. I find it difficult to understand. Going to church and carrying a firearm.

Nicky is changing her career path. She is joining Virgin as a flight attendant. She wants to see the world. She has to sell her pretty home, built and designed to fit on a trailer, and painted candy colours, and move to San Francisco. Virgin have stringent grooming policies, so Nicky will have to keep her tattoos covered (which look stunning and are very colourful) but makeup will not be a problem, as hers is tattooed on, lip gloss, eyebrows and blush. Wow.

Nicky tells me that Donald Trump running for President was initially seen as a joke. Now, it's just plain scary. Wow.

Katie is a travelling nurse. She works in operating theatres, on short-term contracts, all over the USA. She loves to travel. She is also a Warmshowers host. I stayed with her a night, in her house that she is preparing to sell. Being busy sanding floors and painting rooms, and packing for her next adventure, does not stop her hosting cyclists. Katie is also changing her life. She is heading out on her first cycle touring adventure, as soon as the house is on the market, touring the Adriatic. Katie is also looking for a new country to live in. I suggested NZ. I told her we are always open to good looking nurses coming our way. (All our nurses are good looking).

Lenny is an engineer, looking forward to retirement. He is also a Warmshowers host. A good deal of his work time is associated with lawyers on cases dealing with faulty appliances and fittings. Lenny has travelled extensively, including 'snooping' for the army in Afghanistan. He is a cycling enthusiast, but has recently had major surgery on an ankle, so rides his motor bikes, a Harley and a BMW. He sent me the security code for his house, told me to make myself at home, convinced me to stay another day, and then flew off to Atlanta, leaving me alone in his house; such amazing hospitality and trust. In the short time we had together, he took me on a tour of North Charleston, took me out for a pizza, and we got to talk about cycling gadgets, NZ vs. USA, politics, Nepal, law, ACC and OSH, and so much more. Wow.

John describes himself as an Army brat. At sixty-five years old, he has recently finished hiking the Appalachian Trail, and the Pacific Crest Trail. Now he's cycling from Florida to upstate New York. He told me about the dangers of USA, the power of the police, the racism, segregation, and who really cares about USA politics, and how to survive in a Police State. Wow.

The guys at the Statesboro Fire Department greeted me with open arms. I ate a meal with them. We trash talked for hours. Travel, fishing, hunting, cooking, diving, swimming with crocodiles, NZ, sport, NZ sportsmen, legalization of marijuana, Politics and so much more. The Captain prayed for me and told me God was within me. I'm overwhelmed by their generosity and warmth. Then this morning I was ordered to eat the breakfast they had cooked for me. Several are keen to come to NZ to shoot a Red Stag. A couple even sussed out Hanmer Holiday Homes options, and they're serious about coming. Yep, I'm still being wowed.

DOING THE HARD YARDS

29th May 2016

Madray Springs to Folkston 126km
To Maclenny Florida 83km
To Ellaville 113km
To Tallahassee 121km

I'm following the American Adventure Cycling Association maps. They take me on quiet roads, with fantastic scenery. Often, they feel too quiet, with long flats, and little traffic or anything else to distract me, and suddenly it's hot, very hot. I'm looking for people to talk to. I did meet a couple of Aussie cyclists, who for a couple of hours put up with my insistent yakking, and a couple in a diner paid for my breakfast, just to shut me up, but otherwise I'm alone on the road, and it's tough.

But then I met two huge men, father and son, the Sumner family, outside a Piggley Wiggley (a Southern Supermarket chain) and we got talking. Pretty soon I was sent off to meet Miss Libbey, the local newspaper reporter.

The interview started well, but then: *"How far do you ride each day?" "About 60 (90km) to 70 miles (105km), for five or six days then I take a rest day." "I hope that is on Sunday." "I never know what day it will be. I don't even know what day it is today." "But you need to rest on Sunday and worship the maker. What church do you go to?" "My church is the great outdoors." "Well who do you think made it so great and so beautiful? God did. It didn't just happen you know. Do you have a bible?" "Nope." "You need to have one. Your destiny and your salvation lie in the bible. I would give you mine, but it's best to have one in your native language. What is your native language?" "English." "Oh."* I'm not sure whether the article about my adventure will appear in the paper.

I cycle into Madray Springs. There's no one at fire station. The lady in the shop rings someone, who rings someone else. Yes, I can stay at the Fire Station. Great. I put my tent up, but then the Deputy Chief turns up, opens up the station for me. AC, shower, comfortable couch. It's so comfortable, quiet and cool, I sleep well past 7.30am.

Folkston Fire Station. Terry the Chief, *"I know about you. Fire departments all over the south have been alerted. Here is a medal, here is a t-shirt. Help yourself to a shower, washing machine, cold drinks, Internet. Bring your bike inside. What you are doing is amazing. Prostate Cancer. Anything, anything you need, just holler, oh and I'm an All Blacks fan. Played Rugby for US Army all over the world."* I'm totally overwhelmed by the continuous generosity.

And then I turn right, west, towards California, and I get lucky. Friday evening, C Watch in Maclenny has a family meal night. Uncle Stan turns up with 'a gallon of corn, a gallon of green beans, and a couple of gallons of home smoked chicken.' Someone else brings macaroni cheese, and pork steaks. Kids, sisters, grandmas, wives, fire crew and I sit down to a massive feed, and talk. After the excitement of a crazy foreign cyclist, the talk turns to many subjects. I am so privileged to share.

And a sort of reverse inspiration story: Matt is in his mid-thirties and has been in the fire service for ten years. He told me of being an ungrateful lazy kid, stealing from his parents to buy drugs. He became grossly overweight, and was "absolutely a taker", expecting everything given to him. Then at twenty-seven years old his doctor told him his body was shutting down, he was going to die. At the same time, he saw his nephew achieving, training as a Fire-fighter. Matt switched his life around. He lost weight, lots of it. He trained and achieved Fire-fighter I, EMT, and then Fire-fighter II. He joined a volunteer unit and began applying for permanent jobs. He saw fit, strong capable role models in the local brigades, and worked hard to improve his fitness, and eventually was offered a full-time position. The guys he joined on shift had seen his progress, and now used him as inspiration. They all work very hard in the gym, to ensure they will always be able to be there for their buddies in an emergency on the fire scene. A pretty amazing story.

And they are working hard for others as well. Today they raised $2,500 for Muscular Dystrophy and are now halfway to their $10,000 target. And then I arrive in Tallahassee, just missing a close friend, bother. But I meet Lilly and Richie, and extended family, Mother, baby, roommate, and son, and loads of friends who turn up for a BBQ. What an amazing atmosphere. My mother will always tell you, that as a kid, I wanted the whole extended family to live in one house. Here I am, in exactly that situation, and I love it. I couldn't have been made more welcome, more at home, or more part of the furniture. What an awesome USA family experience. On top of that, I got to meet a bunch of mountain bikers who took me out for a ride on Memorial Day Holiday, and they are booking flights to NZ to join me on an mountain bike tour in February or March. Who's coming?

THE STATE OF THE NATION

2nd June 2016

Tallahassee to Carrabelle 121km
To Panama City Beach 134km
To Fort Walton Beach 105km

According to my new mate 'Bill Bytheway', second cousin to my young cycling buddy Charles Brandt Bytheway, the USA is in trouble. One of the big problems is that it is impolite to talk of politics with anyone other than very close friends or family, so no one discusses their real thoughts. At the moment, in the USA, there is a huge debate about transgender toilets in schools. "We should be debating about which idiot is going into the White House, not who goes to what restroom." "And the Bible Belt. Oh boy. Their number plates tell it all, In God we Trust. Well I'm a Christian, but these people need to pull their heads out of the sand (bibles) and get real. If Trump gets into office, I'm going to hide in the woods, behind a big bush, and pray."

Yep, the educated are worried. How many times have I been asked about emigrating to NZ? Lots. And they're serious. But, if you look around, most people seem oblivious, unworried. As if, if they ignore the elephant, it will disappear. But will it?

So, I reluctantly cycled away from my family nest in Tallahassee. Lilly and Ritchie advised me on a route that headed south to the coast, and it was lovely. 25 miles (40km) of cycling along a rail trail, through beautiful forest, then onto Highway 98, all the way to the Gulf of Mexico, and the beaches. Yeeha. Something to look at. I see Pelicans, and Porpoises, and the log of wood on the road turned and sort of hissed at me, before waddling off. My first in-the-wild crocodile, 1.5m long. (Hmmmm. I was going to camp tonight.) I find a cool 'Mom N Pop' Diner, with faux palm trees, real sodas, real jukebox, tall bar stools, small booths, fantastic soup, sandwiches, OJ, and ice-cream, but no waitresses on skates. And I feast. And I end up camping, on a beach. No crocs.

The next day is more of the same, but Highway 98 cuts across a peninsula, and suddenly I'm being assaulted by super jets. This is *Top Gun* country, some of USA's largest Air Force bases, and lots of bright young boys and girls, playing with the world's most expensive toys. Take-offs, landings, scream-pasts. The air is full of very noisy, very fast war planes. My goodness. How many jets do you need? A lot, apparently. And they all need to be in the air at once. And they all need to be at full throttle, and flying really low, and in pairs, so the second one scares you just as much as the first, but before you've recovered from the first scare. If only a fraction of the budget spent on the number of war planes I saw today, was spent on kids' education, there would be some very bright cookies in this country.

Then I hit Panama City. No not another country. Within a couple of hours, I also cycled through Mexico City, and Bahama City. This is Florida's 'Forgotten Coast', and although the beaches are pretty, the rest is pretty tacky. USA resorts at their worst. Hotels and apartments right up to the beach. Access to lots of the beach is private, and behind the hotels? Wide, busy streets lined with mini golf, Ferris wheels, roller coasters, mini race car tracks, junk food outlets, and One Dollar shops.

And for the first time in the USA, I'm turned away from a fire station. Apparently, there are lots of 'bums' on the streets, looking for places to sleep. Instead, I'm sent to a Mission. Here I can register, get a meal, and sleep for free. But, I can't have a shower until after dinner, I must attend a church service, I must not leave the premises after 6pm, I cannot retire to my room, because I haven't got one, and I'm not really comfortable about how secure my stuff will be overnight. What I've been enjoying at fire stations, is the company, the chats, the camaraderie, the sharing of stories. Here, no one talks. Everyone has their own problem, drugs, homeless, bankrupt, alcoholic, or domestic, and they're not sharing. To be honest, I'm very uncomfortable in this atmosphere, and after a couple of hours, still unwashed, decide to move on. There are no campsites, this is resort central, and so for the first time in the USA, I sleep in a Motel.

The further west I go, the less tacky the resorts. In fact, some parts are actually really nice. One area of about 25 miles (40km) has a cycle path along the main road, and it's full of families on bikes; cruisers, trainer wheels, city fold up bikes, skaters, boarders. It's busy. But the buildings are less oppressive, and you can actually see the sea, although access is still not easy. I stop and taste my first frozen custard cone. Yummy. I do find a spot where I'm prepared to lock Fiona and sneak down to the white sand. The water is almost blood temperature, but its clear blue, and refreshing. It would be nice to hang out for a bit, but I can't see Fiona and my gear.

So, I ride on. Everyone seems very relaxed and is enjoying their holiday. No one seems worried. It's only the rest of the world that's saying, "WTF USA?"

MIGHTY MERICAN MILITARY MACHINE

5th June 2016

Fort Walton Beach to Gulf Shores State Park 142km
To Grand Bay 88km
To Waveland Mississippi 117km

For an hour and half traffic streamed towards me. Every vehicle had at least one occupant dressed in military garb. Many had two or three military personnel. Three lanes off heavy traffic, heading to work, on one military base. For ten minutes the traffic flow eased, and then it intensified for another half hour, as another shift started. And during the course of the day, I cycled past three 'military motorways', three lanes roads heading on to military bases. It certainly helps you understand how big the USA military is. It's massive.

As I rode down the coast, at least four different types of military aircraft, did low flybys, patrolling the beaches. For what? Protecting me?

The other day, a local pilot lost his life when his military jet crashed. Flags are flying at half-mast. My mate, Billy Bytheway explains, "I'm not sure whether they're mourning the pilot or the aircraft. The cost of that aircraft would pay the food bill of the nation it was training to bomb for twelve months. A crazy waste of resources."

Bill had lots to say on the military. "The churches around here are really busy on Sundays. The Military, praying for forgiveness, for spending so much of their time learning how to kill." "Defending our country? When was the last time we were attacked? We need to realise that we are the aggressors." "The Corporates and their puppets, the politicians, are the real enemy of the USA." Did I say that Bill was heading to live (hide) in the woods, with his bible?

So, I cycled out of Florida, and into Alabama, where I've been warned there are 'Redneck rednecks'. I get the gist, as I become a plaything for the big wheeled, loud, huge motored trucks. I can hear them coming up behind me, as they cross the rumble lines to get as close as possible to me. I brace myself for the loud "Yeeha" scream of delight as they scare me with another close shave. What fun, NOT.

And a 'City Ordinance' does not allow me to stay at fire stations. However, the local police station is happy for me to camp behind their base. Thanks guys. I'm not so lucky the next night, and am sent to a State Park, where they want me to pay $55.00 for a powered campsite. But I don't want power. But sir, you have a powered site, so it will cost $55.00. Can I have an unpowered site? No sir. That will be $55.00 thank you. No thank you. I will risk the alligators and find somewhere else. I found Bills bush in the woods, and hid out for the night, without a bible, and with my $55.00.

But it rained, heavy rain, with lots of frightening, very close thunder and lightning; frightening, because the first huge clap woke me from a very deep sleep. The rain did lower the temperature, which meant I stopped sweating. It's the small things that you really appreciate.

I was taken in by a Warm Showers family just before the second huge storm. I don't think I've seen so much water falling from the sky before. Fiona wasn't as lucky, but all the sand from the previous night was washed off her. She's just been in for her latest 6,000 miles (10,000km) check. The guys at Bob's Bikes did great work on her rear hub, and those at Ride More Bicycles replaced a few other parts, so Fiona is purring.

And now I'm in Mississippi, at a fire station. Most of the day has been riding past empty building lots, a result of Hurricane Katrina. This coast was really smashed, and is still recovering, eleven years later. Now I'm heading to 'Norleans', hoping to hear some music, and have a couple of days of rest.

THE BIG EASY

9th June 2016

Waveland to New Orleans 92km
To Donaldsonville 133km

The Waveland Fire Station Chief invited me into their air-conditioned accommodation with open arms. Yeeha. It was hot, damn hot. It's okay when you're cycling, as you create a cooling breeze, but stop, and the sweat pours out, like ice melting.

Only two guys are on duty, but it was great chatting to them. One, Marty, is a hunting and fishing enthusiast. The first thing he asked me was about NZ's famous 'Red Stags'. He's very keen to come to NZ to hunt. Like many firemen, these guys have two jobs. Marty works for two fire brigades, in two different cities: sort of like working a shift in Rangiora, then being on call in Kaiapoi on his days off. CJ, his on-duty partner, works with the sheriff's department in Drug Enforcement, on his days off. In the morning he strapped on his gun and deputy badge and went to his second job. I rode into New Orleans.

I stopped at my favourite breakfast stop, The Waffle House, for poached eggs and hash browns, and OJ. Protein, fat, carbohydrate, and vitamins. (Never before have I been so focused on what I'm eating). I had just ordered, and I was joined by a lovely young lady cyclist. Cheyenne is cycling from San Diego and probably to New York. It took her fifty-six days to get to here. She had lots of info to share with me, but other than being lovely company, the best part for me was that she was the first cyclist I've met who has come from my destination. Suddenly, my journey becomes doable. An amazing feeling, and only fifty-six days away. Wow. That's not long. Except, I'm detouring up into Colorado, but for the first time, the end of my journey is within sight.

New Orleans. I wanted to see and hear music, musicians, and feel the vibe of 'the Big Easy'. To be honest, the city weirded me out a bit. One guy told me he "loved Norleans because everyone was really relaxed, and they were able to be themselves". I found myself a little uncomfortable. Lots of homeless, beggars, drunks, people obviously high on drugs, tattooed bodies, dreads, and piercings. Bourbon Street was a bit of a freak show. There is great music, from every bar. I'd love to revisit, but with company. But elderly women dressed in pirate costumes, with their boobs exposed, with Band-Aids covering their nipples, screaming abuse at a guy dressed as a pirate. Was it role play? It looked reasonably serious, and guys vomiting in the gutters, and peeing in public. Nope not where I wanted to be. Jackson Square and Fisherman Street were a lot better, with some amazing bands, and hugely talented performers. However, after two days, and one night walking the very humid streets, my enthusiasm waned. I spent a day in the hostel, sleeping, eating, and watching Netflix. (One and a half seasons of Breaking Bad).

Today, I cycled the Mississippi levee. I've been looking forward to visiting this great river, ever since experiencing the Mekong. It didn't disappoint. Tom Sawyer, Huckleberry Finn and Mark Twain were all in my thoughts. But what I saw were huge ships, 50 miles (80km) from the sea, petroleum plants, and other huge industrial plants, loading and unloading stuff from huge barges on the river, and huge bridges spanning this mighty waterway. When it was time to cross one of these spans, another adventure, a scary one. Lots of fast-moving traffic, with very little room for Fiona and me, and the bridge was very high, and did I say it was hot? But then I found Donaldsonville, and the Donaldsonville Fire Station, and once again was welcomed with open arms. The Emergency Services brotherhood. Amazing.

MY BROTHER WENT TO TENNESSEE ONCE

13th June 2016

Donaldsonville to Krotz Springs 117km
To Oberlin 130km
To Newton Texas 127km
To Silsbee 82km

Louisiana is a lot of swamp, river, and boggy stuff. In fact, some of it is below Sea level. But this makes it very attractive to some of the locals, and many see no reason to travel anywhere, except into the swamps to hunt, Crocs, 'coons, armadillo, fishing and 'froggin'. Apparently when frogging it's best to grab them in your hands, but you can use a net, and give it a flick, so the frog is trapped, then you skin it, and throw it on the grill. But just be aware that skinning the frog on the boat or canoe, and leaving a blood trail, attracts the crocs. Some of the frogs are very big, and I'm sure, very tasty, but I chose not to join them in the dark, in a very narrow canoe, in crocodile waters. Yep I'm chicken. Instead, I stayed at the Firehouse and ate Cajun Chicken, cooked by the Captain. Yum.

The cycling is tough. It's hot, humid hot. I didn't realise fluid could pass through the human body so quickly. Sweat drips out of my hands like a tap. One night, in my tent, I thought I had insects crawling over me. Nope. It was sweat, and I was lying still. My cycling clothes are soaked within five minutes of getting on the bike. After 60 miles (100km) today, for the first time in an awfully long time, my backside was raw from chaffing. For the next 12 miles (20km) I couldn't sit. Very uncomfortable.

But I love the locals. Every time I stop, I'm asked questions. Often, they've got no idea of where NZ is, but just telling them I'm cycling to California astounds them. I met John. He cycled across the south a couple of years ago, with six others, writing and performing a play as they travelled. He's also been to Christchurch, travelling with the Coast Guard to Antarctica. Lots of common ground to chat about and I was glad for the break.

I'm in a Firehouse eating a meal with sixteen adults. They are enthusiastically asking me about my travel. But I'm interested in their stories. I ask, *"What about you? Where have you guys travelled?"* There is quiet in the room. Eventually one pipes up with: *"My brother went to Tennessee once."* None of them had travelled out of the state, nor had any plans to do so. *"Why would we go anywhere else? We have jobs, women and the hunting and fishing's great."*

It's been raining heaps, but that's good. It's refreshing, and cooling, but when it stops, it's steamy. My glasses keep fogging up from steam off the wet road.

There's been a lot of rain here in Texas lately. A couple of weeks ago they had 15" (40cm) in two hours. The Newton Fire brigade spent over twenty-four hours rescuing people. The station was in disarray, and before I had even realised, the Captain had booked and paid for me to stay in a local motel. Wow. Then the motel owner took frozen pizza from her freezer for me and wouldn't let me pay. I was warned about Texas hospitality.

"You can't cycle across Texas", was another warning, from my mate Bill Dvorak. Now that's a challenge, but he might know a thing or two. I'm exhausted. I've stopped for a day. Sleeping and eating, and enjoying the AC.

THE SOUTH - IMPRESSIONS

18th June 2016

Silsbee to Shepard 102km
To Richards 101km
To Carmine 116km
To Austin 35km (70km Hitched)

I stopped for a break at the Thicket General Store. The owner was a lovely guy and came and sat with me to drink his coffee. *"So, this is Texas, and we're surrounded by a bunch of small, insignificant satellite states, called the United States. What are your feelings about our elections?"*. I wished him and the USA luck. *"This is the worst choice I've had in fifty years of voting. I'm going over to that church on November 8th and voting for Trump. Then I'm coming back here to my store, and drinking mouth wash, because I'm going to have a mighty bad taste in my mouth."* I'm meeting some lovely people, and they're talking to me, and it's great. And I'm getting some interesting impressions of 'the South'. It's certainly a very different USA to that I've experienced before. Impressions include:

The people are friendly and interested. So many don't know where NZ is. "Where'd you ride that there sickle from?" NZ. "Where you riding it too"? LA. "Y'all riding that there sickle from here to California. Oh, my Lord."

There are soooo many overweight people.

There are soooo many grossly overweight people.

There are motorized karts in supermarkets for the overweight people.

The choice in supermarkets is huge, with whole aisles of cereals, all incredibly sugary. There is little choice in service stations, either sweet or deep fried, or both.

On the 'shootings' issue: Blame Obama. Blame ISIS. Blame the Democrats. Blame Muslims. Don't mention 'Gun laws'.

There are some amazing plantation mansions that are preened and groomed like golf courses. In fact, many houses have areas the size of half a dozen rugby fields that are immaculately groomed, and next door are trashed up hovels, surrounded by junk. Both are being lived in. There are a huge number of people who live in relocatable homes.

You can rank the extent of 'Red Neckness' by someone's truck. Big wide wheels: redneck. Big wide wheels and huge muffler: dedicated redneck. Big wide wheels, huge muffler, and vehicle jacked up to expose pretty coloured suspension: extreme redneck.

Gallons, fluid ounces, Yards and Miles, weight in pounds and ounces. It's not easy. But so many of these folks are lovely, keen to chat, and pass on the time of the day.

Maybe it's the heat. It slows everything down. No one is in a rush. You just get hot and sweaty and trust me I know about that. I'm struggling to cycle 70 miles (100km) a day. I lay on my mattress in the tent, dripping in sweat, not sleeping. The other night, at midnight, I was still not asleep. There was a huge moon. I packed everything up, and cycled for two hours, until the moon disappeared. It was very cool compared to the daytime, but I was attacked twice by dogs, and dodged numerous snakes and scorpions warming themselves on the still warm road, damn. I made 20 miles (32km), and then pitched my tent until dawn. Trouble was it stuffed my rhythm for the next day. I was knackered.

I had a rare chance to clean and groom myself up the other night. For several weeks, I've noticed a couple of moles, growing fast, one on my shoulder blade, and one on my calf. A careful look at them reveals that they are not moles, but ticks. Oooops. I enlist the assistance of a National Guardsman staying at the same motel, to help extract them. Fire and Brimstone, and Ticks. Welcome to the South.

Over two years, I've had as few as six punctures. Then the other day, I got two within an hour, big ones, a huge piece of shredded glass, and a pinch, going over a rail line. I spent some time repairing both. But I'm not sure whether it's the heat, the glue, or my patching skills, but both tyres keep blowing the patches off. Yesterday, I'm 30 miles (50km) from Austin, on a major highway. It was very hot. Within a couple of miles, I had three flat tyres. Result. I'm out of patches, glue and patience. I stick put my thumb. And now we see the 'true South'. In India, Nepal, Myanmar, Iran, Turkey, Vietnam, Indonesia, and more, there would have been people stopping to help me before I had my tool kit out. In the South, where over half the vehicles roaring past me are 'pickups' with empty decks, it seems everyone is too busy, or too afraid of their own shadows, to stop and help what is obviously a cyclist in distress. For over half an hour I stood in the beating heat (45C) before three angels turned around and picked me up. I cried. I also cried when they took me to a bike shop and bought me two new tubes. And I cried a third time, when they drove me to the door of my host's house. Thank you thank you thank you, Angels Lisa, John and Mike. You restored my faith in the South.

ROBERT, SUSAN, GORDON & JAMES

19th June 2016

Austin Texas

Oh, how wonderful, to find a sanctuary, somewhere out of the heat, where I can rest and regroup, mend punctures, sleep and eat. Susan was a client on a Hiking NZ trip just before I left home, and she offered me her home as a resting spot. Initially she and Robert were away, but I was told where keys were hidden, how to turn on AC and Netflix, and where the nearest supermarket was, should I run out of all the food Susan had left me. I cried as I entered the house. The heat, punctures, and miles have knocked me and I'm tired.

Two days later, Susan and Robert return, to find me watching season three of Breaking Bad, the fridge empty, but my washing is done, and I'm feeling a good deal more rested. They have now offered to be my local guides. It's so good having a local show you around. I had been out once, to the supermarket, driving Roberts's truck. Wow. That was an adventure. Trying to navigate, stay on the right side of the road, and remember road rules. And then I lost the truck in the supermarket car park. Hmmmm. What colour was it? Cycling is so much easier.

But what has Austin got to offer? I've been told that it is a city of Democrats, in a State (Texas) of Republicans, and that sort of distinction is huge here in the USA. We went walking. Wow. There are heaps of cyclists, runners, and walkers in this city. I've seen nothing like it since Winston Salem and New York. There are cycle tracks, walking paths, lots of cycle rental places, skateboarders, and footpaths. Just four days ago, I had to walk on the road from my motel to a supermarket, because there was no 'pavement'. Austin is very different. People are using public transport. Many inner-city residents don't own cars. If they need to go to a supermarket, they use a local shared-vehicle service, something like Uber. These guys are definitely thinking differently to most the rest of the South.

I visited a barber. I've enjoyed comparing barbers around the world. These guys were great, dressed in white shirts and ties, and very professional, and personable, interested in my story, and sharing their stories. It cost a $15.00, more expensive than the $2.00 Nepali haircut, but a very pleasant experience.

And did you know Austin has music, as well as an incredibly active outdoor pursuits scene? Almost every night, one of half a dozen busy music venues, has a famous artist performing. Tuesday night is Gordon Lightfoot. In my university days, way back in the 1970s, we spent many a night relaxing with a wine or beer, in front of an open fire, as he crooned in the background. Gotta go, because we can.

The Austin City Limits Moody Theatre is an amazing venue. It has been used by many, many famous recording artists for live recordings. Willy Nelson has performed here 3,333 times. We sat just above stage right, very close to Gordon. I have to say, that at seventy-seven years old, his voice hasn't got the vibrancy of his youth, but his songs brought back lots of memories, the atmosphere was amazing, the crowd boisterous, especially the lady just in front of us, and it certainly felt very special to be at such an amazing venue. (Lots of ideas for improving the Hanmer Springs hall).

So, I'm ready to hit the road again. But wait a minute. Wednesday night. James Taylor is performing. I'm here. He's here. Damn. Sorry guys. I might be a day late catching up with you in Denver, San Diego, Los Angeles (oops, not LA. I'm meeting Ju there. I'll be on time, honey).

TOUGH OR STUPID

26th June 2016

Austin to Fredericksburg 135km
To Guadalupe River Valley 82km
To Camp Wood 96km
To Brackettville 82km

I'm climbing up a hill. I haven't seen many until just the last few days. I'm hurting. I'm soaked in sweat. It's steep, hot and ugly. At the top is a picnic area, and there are a bunch of Harley riders taking in the view. One of the women says to me: *"Man. Yous my hero. That was a killer hill."* I reply: *"No lady. I'm no hero. I'm just a stupid old man, trying to cycle around the globe."* Such is the dilemma I'm facing every day, as I attempt to cycle across Texas.

I reluctantly cycled away from the haven that was Robert and Susan's home, away from AC, good food, wonderful company, and amazing music. James Taylor was fantastic. I cycle away with warnings about the heat, dehydration, and traffic conditions. It's hot, but there is a slight breeze, that takes the worst of the heat away, as long as you keep cycling. My route takes me along reasonably quiet roads, with shade trees, so in fact it's quite pleasant. I'm drinking heaps, mostly all with electrolytes added. I should be okay. But my mistake today, yep I'm still making them after 760 days on the road, was deciding to make it to Fredericksburg. My map told me it was 75 miles (110km). In fact, it was 85 miles (130km), and I was stuffed by the time I got there. To be fair, there were very few places where I might have camped. The roads are bordered by 8ft fences, and 'No Trespassing' signs. To add to my woes, the Fire brigade wouldn't let me camp on their land. No one was prepared to make a decision without the Chiefs okay. I was sent to a campsite, via a supermarket, 3 miles (5km) out of town.

The shopping wasn't too successful. I was too tired, and hungry to think straight. At the campsite, I got my tent up, and crashed out, too tired to eat. But that's when the cramps started. I couldn't roll over without another part of my body cramping. Damn. Hadn't I drunk enough? I tossed and turned until midnight, when I had enough energy to eat some cheese and crackers, and then I slept until 8am. Hmmmm. Lessons learnt. I hope.

The next day was tough. There was still a slight breeze, but my body was shot. Every 6 miles (10km), I got off my bike to drink, lie down beside the road, and sleep, then wake and drink again, climb back on the bike and struggle on.

Once I woke to see buzzards circling above me. Hmmmm. By 40 miles (70km) I'm looking for somewhere to camp. By 50 miles (80km), I've had enough. A shady tree, 5m from the road, exposed for all to see, is the best I can find, but I can't go any further. It's 6pm, and I'm asleep within minutes of crawling inside the tent, and don't hear a thing until I wake at 6am.

Day three and its overcast, with a slight breeze. Now this is better. It even rains slightly once or twice. At one rest stop, a Hummingbird fits around me, examining my GrumGoesGlobal yellow flag. Twice I'm inspected by a huge Red-Tailed Eagle. A young deer buck with a beautiful set of velvety antlers bounds across the road in front of me. Later, a doe and fawn cross in front of me. The doe leaps over a fence, but the fawn can't jump it, so runs along it, until it finds an overhanging tree, that it thinks it's hidden behind. I hope it found its mother. Buzzards congregate in groups, as they gorge on deer and other roadkill. They are very reluctant to fly away, after all, I'm only a cyclist, and seemingly offer very little threat. I see my first porcupine (roadkill), and a Roadrunner (but no Wile E. Coyote). I'm almost enjoying the ride today.

Then I hit a junction, and I'm joined by hundreds of motorcyclists. The road is up and down, twisting and turning and just what the Harley and Goldwing Clubs love for their Saturday ride. It's not so much fun on a bicycle. But the motorcyclists give me lots of encouragement, secret waves, raised fists, thumbs up. Several car clubs are also out cruising. They also give me loud cheers and waves. (A few of my Petrol Head mates would have been drooling just to see them, but I didn't even have a chance to get photos, sorry).

I stop at a General Store. The local policemen, and the storekeeper, have a competition, trying to outdo each other on the ugliness ahead of me. Big hills, hot, dry, ugly critters, prickly plants, grumpy landowners. I'm told "sensible cyclists cross Texas in Spring or Fall". As if it wasn't tough enough. Oh well. How stupid am I? Only 400miles (700km) to El Paso, then another 500 miles (800km) to San Diego.

THE HEAT BEAT ME, BILL

30th June 2016

Brackettville to Seminole Canyon 130km
To Dryden 100km
To El Paso (Bus 350km 5 hours)
To Denver (Bus 1000+km 15 hours)

I've jumped on a couple of buses, and got out of the heat, and Texas. Bill told me, "You can't ride across Texas", and he was right. It was hot, damn hot, and it was killing me.

I had a reasonably good day out of Brackettville. The temperature started cooler, and it was overcast, and the miles clicked past. But by the time I got to Seminole Canyon State Park, it was really hot again, 105°F. Here was a chance to camp, cheaply and safely, and really close to the Rio Grande and Mexico, 3 miles (5km). I was too tired to walk to the Rio Grande, the border between two countries, but decided Fiona might be able to manage the trip, unloaded. She did great. The trail was sandy and rocky, but it seems as if my mountain biking skills have left me, although I only fell off once. I was too busy looking for snakes to see the deep sand, and the slippery slanting rock. Oh well.

My body seems drained, exhausted. I've been finding it really hard to eat. Nothing in the rest stops looks appetizing, and when I do buy something, I can only eat small amounts. It's a real worry. The last week or so have been a huge effort to get on to the bike, the first time on my global journey I haven't been excited about cycling today. I pretty sure it's the heat. And now I've got diarrhoea. Bother.

Today I met Leo. He has cycled out of Denver and is heading to Florida. It has taken him two weeks. He looks beat. He has a badly sunburnt face, burnt lips, and complains of the head wind and the heat. Meeting him perks me up, as I'm sure I don't look as bad as he does, and I haven't seen cyclists in a while.

I also meet a young man walking across the USA, pushing his stuff in a pram. Very brave. And I'm stopped at a Border Control checkpoint. For the first time since Central Asia I have to produce my passport when I'm not actually crossing a border. There are Border Patrol vehicles everywhere in this area. Down dusty back roads, in riverbeds, patrolling the highway, at all times of the day and night. My tent is spotlighted in the early hours of the morning.

There is a vehicle waiting for me to emerge from the campsite, just checking I'm not an illegal. The only buses I see are labelled 'Detention Centre', and they are filled with Mexicans.

I'm hoping for a better day cycling after a good night's sleep at the State Park, but even at 6am it's hot, and I'm feeling really weak. I struggle all day. I'm told its 105°F, then 110°F, then a little later, 115°F. There is very little shade. I stop at a picnic area, with a covered table. An American Chinese family offer me watermelon. They are very concerned that I'm out in the heat, but their vehicle is packed. I'm offered water, which I've got plenty of, and they leave. I fall asleep on the table. Bother.

I drag myself back on the bike, and eventually make it to Dryden, and the General Store. I am saved. I collapse on a chair, in front of the AC. A lovely family tends to my needs. Cold drinks, food, and advice. I'm not going any further today, what are my options. I can camp behind the store. I can sleep in their camper. And can wash under a hose. They introduce me to some locals, there are only eight residents in this "town", and they all offer advice. I could catch a train, but it is often delayed, very late, or cancelled. I could catch a bus, but its schedule is also very erratic. Then Pat offers to give me a ride in the morning, to a larger town, on a bigger highway, where he is certain the buses west are more regular. Yeeha. I accept; maybe the first sensible decision for some days.

Pat and his wife are retired Army. They farm ducks, chickens, and goats, and have thirteen dogs. Pat wears a revolver in his jeans pocket. For an hour, I'm intrigued by Pats stories, of secret military missions, conflicts with Border Patrol, lawsuits against the state, testing of biological weapons, and lots more. Pat is not only very knowledgeable, but also has some amazing stories, and is great company, and he helped me out of a deep hole I had got myself into. I love small-town people.

Pat drops me at a Burger King/Service Area that doubles as a bus depot. The ladies behind the counter are not very helpful.

"Sir, a non-refundable bus ticket to El Paso costs $83.00."

'Or you could buy a ticket for $98.00, which allows you to alter which bus you travel on, if you pay an extra $20.00."

'Sir, I'm unsure whether you can take your bicycle. You will have to ask the driver."

I decide to spend the three hours before the bus arrives trying to hitch a ride. I get offered money twice. I am offered prayers. I am abused twice for interrupting. I am not offered a ride, although I ask only those seemingly heading in my direction, and with empty pickup trucks. Hmmmm.

The first bus driver: "*Nope. You can't take a bike on the bus unless it's in a box.*" Where am I going to get a box big enough at a Service Area?

The second bus driver:" *Put cardboard around these parts, and I will let you on my bus, but be quick. I leave in ten minutes.*" Yeeha. A mad dash. I find empty chip boxes. I wrap the offending parts, and bungee the cardboard on. I don't care whether it stays on, after the luggage door is closed. I buy an $83.00 ticket, with the driver breathing over my shoulder. The unhelpful lady's computer is not connecting, and she abuses me and the bus driver for putting her under pressure. We depart, only five minutes behind schedule. I'm 'jumping' 220 miles (350km), across Texas, to El Paso. Then I'm getting another bus 700 miles (1,100km) north, and hopefully out of the heat.

I LOVE COLORADO

7th July 2016

Denver Colorado to Idaho Springs 75km
To Loveland Ski Resort 50km
To Dvoraks Centreville 169km

It was a long night trying to get comfortable enough to sleep in the bus seat, and even more difficult when the seat next to me was occupied at about 1am, but the fourteen hours and 700 miles (1100km) were worth it. Stretching our legs in Trinidad Colorado at 6am, for the first time in weeks the air was fresh and cool. Oh, Colorado, I love you.

Unpacking Fiona and the trailer took only a short while, and we were off navigating through Denver to the home of my amazing Denver family, Scott, Sarah, and Mira. How wonderful to be able to kick back and relax in a family atmosphere again. So many little things that you miss while touring on a bicycle; running water, electricity, food in the fridge, lounging on a couch, the same bed more than one night in a row, and lots and lots of catching up, and frank discussions, and the chance to cook a real meal. All things that most of us take for granted but have been denied to me for what seems an awfully long time. We even managed a couple of family hikes in surrounding mountain parks, and I got to share a 4th of July family barbecue. I truly did not want to leave.

But I did, heading towards the Rockies. For the next 120 miles (200km) I cycled on sealed cycle paths, or very seldom used 'frontage roads', the old highways that parallel the motorways, really pleasant cycling. Crossing Texas, I took maybe thirty photos. Here in Colorado, in three days, I've taken almost 150 photos. There is scenery to die for, and I needed lots of breaks, as the climbing had started. Remembering Denver is a mile high, and I was heading towards the Continental Divide, you can imagine that sometimes the going was tough. I was back to cycling 100m, and sometimes only 50m, before having to stop to catch my breath, and let my heart rate slow. I'm at altitude again. The scenery is stunning, and there are plenty of other cyclists about. Some who ignore me, but many others who chat, and give encouragement, though none pulling a load like Fiona carries.

My legs were pretty shot by the time I got to Idaho Springs, and I had to squeeze in between the crowds of holidaying families to get a pretty yummy pizza. So, it seemed like a good place to find somewhere to camp, and recoup before the climb tomorrow. I found a spot just out of town, just off the cycle track, and slept. Soundly.

Juliet and I had driven through this way three years ago, on our mountain biking trip, and I wanted to cycle through here as soon as I saw the terrain, so it became part of my 'must do' route, and it took me from the home of my Denver family to the home of my Rockies family, over a couple of hills that excited me. But I had some tough climbing to do before I got close enough to challenge the passes. Day two was slow. 30 miles (50km) and I was exhausted. I begged some water from a closed ski area and pitched my tent in a small patch of bush opposite their car park.

Loveland Pass. 11,990 feet (3600m). It's back to basics. Small steps, but the scenery and colours early in the morning were stunning, so the breaks were used for more than just catching my breath. Did I tell you I love Colorado? The elation on reaching the top was pretty special. I haven't climbed like this since Andorra. And the downhill, and breakfast in Keystone were pretty good too. It's amazing how a win raises your spirits. I'm back on sealed cycle paths, all the way into Frisco, for a smoothie, and then climbing again towards Copper Mountain. I meet several cyclists who are very encouraging, while dodging hundreds of out of control families of cyclists, who have been set loose by bike companies at the top of the hill. I know they haven't cycled up this path. And then I turn left, away from the crowds. I'm the only cyclist heading up Freemont Pass. More tiny steps.

Fremont Pass (11,383 feet) and the 'town' of Climax, where a very special mineral, that I can't spell or pronounce, is mined. It is used to harden steel. I've climbed my two hills for the day and am feeling pretty chuffed. It's downhill to Leadville, a very cool little town on the side of a mountain. It's 5pm, as I sup a smoothie. Where to stay? Damn it. It's 37 miles (65km) to Dvorak's, and it's downhill, and I've got three hours daylight. Let's do it.

103 miles (169km), two 11,000-foot passes, and I'm welcomed by big hugs and smiles. What could be a better way to end an amazing day? The next two days I get to mix with the rafting crew, help with shuttles, help Bill put up signs for his election campaign, to become Chaffee County Commissioner, and go out for an amazing Mexican meal. I'm at home again, with my Rockies Family. Did I mention that I love Colorado?

WHO CHOSE THIS ROUTE?

12th July 2016

Dvoraks to Sargeant 75km
To Stevens Creek 64km
To Montrose 90km

Once again, I didn't really want to leave somewhere I feel really comfortable.
The Dvorak's were off on a Gunnison fishing trip with clients, and though I
could have stayed around and helped with shuttles, I've still got a few miles to
go, and time is getting short. Only five weeks until Ju arrives. So, it's back on
the bike and on the road.

Downhill for 10 miles (16km) to start the day, yippee, and then the climb
started. Hmmmm. I've linked up a very interesting route, but who knew
it would have me crossing the Continental Divide three times. Monarch
Pass (11,312'). I can't tell a lie. It was tough. So much for being acclimated
(acclimatised), a slow painful grind, and with very little shoulder, and lots
of speeding traffic. But I made it, and was grinning widely; so much so, that
quite a few people spoke to me. In 2013, Ju and I had come here to ride the
Monarch Crest Trail and had been chased by a huge thunderstorm. No storm
today, but it felt great to be in a familiar place. So familiar, that I was able
to advice a small group of very pleasant people from Denver on good local
places to mountain bike and eat. (Once a guide always a guide).

Just over the top, after a huge ice cream, I met a young lady cyclist, from
Hildenborough, Kent where we used to live. She was five years older than
my kids, so we figured she must have gone to the same school as Lisa and
Paul, when they were five and six years old; small world. She was cycling
the Western Express, the route I'm about to join, and had taken about three
weeks to get to the top of Monarch Pass. Oh, my goodness. In three weeks,
I could be on the Pacific Coast. I will have all but (just got to get to Hanmer
Springs), made a complete circuit of the globe. Wow. We chatted for some
time, and then I enjoyed a mighty fine downhill. But what's this? A very, very
strong head wind. I find a sheltered spot and make camp. I'm knackered.

The wind is supposed to only blow in the afternoon, but not today. I struggle
into it for six hours and make 35 miles. I find a State Camping area and try
to find a sheltered spot. I pitch the tent. Inside the tent it's sweltering hot.
Outside, it's blowing a gale, and nasty Red Ants are all over my feet, and
biting. I decide on a luggage free cycle down to the lake edge. Oh heck!!! The

Red Ants are all over my helmet, in my hair, down my neck, into my arm pits, looking for moisture. Aaaarrrhhhh. The lake is too far away. It's a sprint to the freshwater tap, and lots of rapid splashing and slapping. Nasty, nasty, nasty. Once again, I sleep really well.

I awake at 3am. There's no wind. Shall I pack up and ride? Hmmmm. Memories of the scorpions, rattle snakes, and feral dogs that inhabited the highways of Texas at night. I think I'll sleep another couple of hours. 6am and I'm away. It's very cool. Last night it was necessary to dig out my sleeping bag. I could really do with finding my full finger gloves, but there's no wind. I want to get as far as possible before it begins to blow about noon. The scenery is still spectacular, and I meet two female cyclists from Ireland. They've taken nineteen days from San Francisco. Then I meet a guy from San Francisco. He's taken twenty-eight days. I'm confused, but I'm on track. I stop at a cute General Store for eggs on toast. I climb two long hills, and then it's a long downhill of about 15 miles (20kms) into Montrose. It's only midday, but I'm happy to stop. I've beaten the wind, just. It's a struggle putting the tent up, as it's blowing hard. Yes, a good decision, recharging myself and electronics, washing clothes and my smelly body, shopping, eating, and chatting to a family from Quebec. A great afternoon.

I chose the route. It was tough, but every day on this adventure has been a challenge. Let it continue, for about another month.

THE MILLION-DOLLAR HIGHWAY

14th July 2016

Montrose to Million Dollar Highway 77km
To Durango 109km

Since before I cycled out of Hanmer Springs in 2014, there have been only a few 'must do' places I wanted to cycle to.

Kathmandu was the first, and a bonus was to find that Belinda and Nick were living there.

Second my cousins in North Carolina—I had been promising to visit them for close to thirty years. Though they never really expected me to turn up on their doorstep in Winston Salem on my bicycle.

Visiting my fantastic friends Sarah and Scott in Denver was always going to be part of this amazing journey.

Dvorak' Expeditions just out of Salida, have been a big part of my life for twenty years, and to be able to cycle there via Leadville has been a long-time dream.

In 2013, Juliet and I drove over the road from Durango to Montrose. We had been chased out of Durango by a massive storm and drove through some stunning snow-covered scenery. I had to come back.

Ju and I met Ted and Moira while Mountain biking at Phil's World, between Durango and Cortez. They invited us to spend an evening with them; great food, an amazing 'pallet bonfire' and great company. Ju must have impressed them, because I was invited back. They are looking after me now.

Visiting Annie in San Diego has also been a goal; the only one yet to achieve.

The Million Dollar Highway, between Montrose and Durango must be one of the most beautiful highways in the world. I'd been warned repeatedly that it was dangerous, steep, no roadside railings, with crazy, incapable tourists driving unsafely while looking at the views, but I disregarded all the warnings, and survived. I only had one close call, a concrete mixer truck, claiming more road than necessary, just out of Montrose. During the rest of the ride I met only lovely people. At the summits of the passes, many came to chat.

The senior lady mountain biker at a cafe, who told me she had just bought her eighty-year-old husband an E Bike, so he could keep up with her.

The two guys from the Congo, who were driving a yellow school bus to Texas that had overheated. "We should have stayed on the Freeway but decided to take a short cut. New Zealand? Is that in Europe? Near Austria?"

The Harley riders who were aghast at my ability to cycle up the hills. "How the hell do you do that?" My answer? "Slowly."

The guy who played in the Tauranga Boys High School 2nd XV when he was an exchange student.

The other guy who cycled NZ with his wife many years ago and loved it.

Another guy who had cycled the South Island, chaining his bike to a tree so as he could hike the trails in Arthurs Pass.

The Fire-fighter/EMT from Fairplay, who passed through Christchurch, and loved it, on her way to McMurdo, near Scott Base. She's promising to visit again, next year.

The Texans who had just spent the weekend quad biking on the Alpine Loop. I talked to them at a roadworks traffic light. The traffic controller sent me through the roadworks first. I beat the Texans to a breakfast Cafe 13 miles (25km) downhill; it was very cold. They came into the cafe really surprised to see me and we chatted some more, while they ordered. When their order arrived, they all took off their caps, thanked the Lord, in a very long prayer, for their food, put their caps back on and scoffed. They just hadn't seemed the type to 'give thanks'.

I didn't see one other cyclist going over the highway, except a couple of road bikers in the foothills. Perhaps they've been scared off by the warnings. It was tough. Three passes, all around 11,000 feet. It was steep. There was plenty of traffic, but mostly it was friendly. I rested frequently. I took small steps. And I'm really glad I did it. But it was stunning; absolutely stunning: The Million Dollar Highway. Tick.

DOLORES

18th July 2016

Durango to Dolores 82km
To Bluff Utah 130km
To Kane Gulch 82km

Dolores reminds me of a big pink pig from Wal Footrot's farm. I'm tired, and I'm really missing my involvement in community stuff at home. I'm very close to finishing this epic adventure, yet still have many miles to cycle, and once again, I'm cycling away from a place where I was treated so well, where I felt comfortable, and could have stayed a lot longer.

Ted and Moira cycled with me for 6 miles (10km) out of the city. That was really nice. But it was a little sad, when they turned back towards home, and it was very sad that I had to climb a hill alone as soon as they left. Bother. But things looked up, as I headed down the other side. The scenery was really pleasant, and the traffic not too heavy.

I cycled into the small town of Mancos, where I found a Cafe/Bakery that served a very nice tomato soup, with fresh bread and butter. Yum, just what I needed. People in Colorado are very interested in my journey, and it's really nice to talk to them. Often, when the cycling is tough, these contacts are the high point of a day. It's really encouraging when these folk 'wow' at my achievement and wish me luck for the continuation of the journey. It happened twice here in Mancos. Thank you all.

So, I turned right into Dolores. I needed to find some supplies. I had been here before, way back in 1995, when on a Staff Training Rafting trip. The town looks different today. The first person I meet is Jerry. He's riding a tricycle across the USA. Really interesting to chat, and as we are heading in the same direction, we may meet again. He tells me to visit Lizardhead Cyclery in Dolores and chat to the owner.

"Hi. Do you want some free food? Do you need water? Can I help you with your bike?" This is Lindsay from Lizardhead, an amazingly generous and amenable young man. I eat, refill water, and we chat. He introduces me to one of his customers, Alex. She asks, *"Would you like to come and stay at our house? We have a small studio you can use. My husband loves to chat to cyclists."*

I've only done 50 miles (80km), but it sounds like a great offer. Alex once trained at Dvorak'. Now she is the mother of six-year-old twins. She also helps organise the Dolores River Festival, a music festival based around river activities. Chris, her husband, is an EMT and Fire-fighter, and a Massage Therapist. It seems as if there might be enough common interests to keep a conversation going. I had a lovely evening, staying up far too late. Heaps of ideas exchanged, and subjects discussed. Thank you heaps, you wonderful people.

7.45am and I'm outside the Dolores Grocery. The owner comes out to tell me he will be open in fifteen minutes. Inside I stock up on food. I'm going to be a little remote over the next week or so. As I'm packing, the owner comes out to chat. *"Which way are you going? Have you considered this route?"* He produces some maps, and advises me to head towards Bluff, instead of the regular Western Express route. Funnily enough, Chris had suggested this last night. I decide to take their advice.

Downhill to Cortez, and along beside the San Juan River, the route is very scenic, and very quiet. I've done 50 miles (80km) before I see my first service area. The Trading Post, which should have been open just near the Colorado/Utah border, was closed. I rest. Ice-cream, lollies, and three litres of juice, and a power nap, and I'm ready to try for Bluff. Bluff is one of many huge red rock formations. They are stunning, but I'm exhausted. I crawl into the small town, find a campsite, and a steakhouse (barbecue chicken), and sleep, despite the windstorm

My advisers have sent me north, via Moki Dugway. This is a spot near the top of one of these amazing bluffs. Trouble is, when listening to their directions, I'm not sure I registered just how much a climb I was expected to cycle. I reckon 1500 feet, mostly on gravel (which I got), with huge drop offs (which I saw). Hmmmm. Lots of passers-by tooted or yelled encouragement. Some stopped to offer water. Many voiced amazement at the crazy old man from NZ, attempting such a horrific feat. Some stopped to ensure I was okay, when they saw me power napping at the side of the road. None offered a lift. In truth, it wasn't as hard as some of the climbs I've tackled in the last couple of years, but it was challenging, and the scenery was amazing.

I need to do some more miles, and my legs are shot. The next 20 miles (32kms) were really hard. Initially it was very hot, and then it rained, well poured really, with lots of thunder and lightning, and heavy, drenching rain. Then it got hot again, and the road just went up and down like a roller coaster. Eventually, I could go no more. I found a small side road, and camped above a 'gulch', on a rock shelf, above a canyon. I reckon I will sleep well yet again.

MAJESTIC UTAH

21st July 2016

Kane Gulch to Hog Springs 108km
To Fruita Utah 118km
To Torrey 30km

I've been to Utah several times before, rafting and mountain biking, and driving through, and each time I've been impressed with how awesome the scenery is, but cycling through adds another level of awesome. On the lonely roads I'm cycling, I can be alone for up to an hour with the towering Buttes, and the mighty canyons. I feel miniscule, in wonder at the magnitude and the magnificence, slowly weaving my way, over, beneath, and eventually, past, the majesty.

Today I'm passed by a group of about thirty souped-up sporty cars. They've all got a sticker on the door, as if they're in some sort of rally. I'm pretty sure they're the same cars that raced past me on the Million Dollar Highway. Difference here in Utah, is that they've got a very large Police escort, Motor Bike Cops, Sheriff Cars, and flashing lights.

I meet two 'American' cyclists. He is from Boston. She is from Mexico City. She loves the cycling and feels she may want to go beyond the East coast of the USA, but she wants to ask questions of any other solo female cycle tourers. He is having trouble with his knees, and wonders whether he will make Virginia.

A little later, I meet father and son from Perth. They've only got a three-month visa and want to get to New York. I advised them to not fret about schedules, enjoy the ride, and get a bus if they run out of time. Hmmmm. Perhaps I should heed my own advice. I've got 1000 miles (1600km) to go to Pacific Coast, and only twenty-three days before Ju arrives.

I was feeling pretty chirpy when I met the Aussies. I was cruising down a very long hill. Fiona hums going downhill, but today there is a different tune, bother. My trailer has a puncture. Many people ask whether the trailer affects my ride. Honestly, I often have to look behind me to ensure I have connected it. And then I forget to do maintenance on it. The tyre has worn through beyond the threads. The tube is sticking out. Bother. A couple of layers of Duct tape should get me to the next Bike Shop in Cedar City. That tyre only lasted 3000 miles (5000km), from Lisbon. Others have lasted twice that distance.

I rest for a couple of hours at a very small shop at Hite, out of the heat, eating ice cream. Then I get to cross the Colorado River. I wasn't sure I would see it on this trip. I climb a sharp short incline to a rest area. I'm stuffed. (Too much ice cream). There is no sign forbidding camping, but it is signposted 'Rest Area Only'. I cycle to the very back, and rest. Just before dark, I stretch my sleeping mat out on a picnic table, under a shelter. I'm not camping. I'm resting, and then the storm starts, huge thunder, dazzling lightening, and for several hours. I can't sleep for the noise and flashes.

Next day, and I'm carrying 15l of fluid, and having to ration my intake in case I run out. It's hot. But I'm on a familiar road. Juliet and I drove this road three years ago on our mountain biking tour. It leads me to Fruita, Utah, and a National Park. I have to stay at a designated campsite, $20.00. But it's all but full. I negotiate with a young motorcyclist to share his site, although it's not the done thing; it allows a Dutch family in a campervan to have my site, instead of driving another couple of hours. Whatever. Once again, I'm knackered.

Up early and straight away I'm climbing. Damn. My legs are shot. My whole body is tired. It's not as if I haven't been eating, drinking or sleeping. I need a rest. 20 miles (32km) gets me to Torrey, where I eat a second breakfast. Afterwards I still feel knackered. A guy on a bicycle is looking at Fiona. *"Can you tell me where I might find some cheap accommodation?" "Sure. Follow me."* We cycle a few hundred metres. *"You may as well come to my place. I've cycle toured in NZ. They really looked after me."* Thank you, NZ. Paying it forward.

PIONEER DAY

25th July 2016

Torrey to Hogsback Ridge 72km
To Tropic 100km
To Panguitch Lake 80km
To Cedar City 60km

On July 24th in 1847, the founding father of the Mormon Church said of the Salt Lake Valley, "This is the right place." Ever since then 24th July has been a holiday - Pioneer Day - in Utah. Who knew?

I was enjoying the unexpected, but very much appreciated, hospitality of Chris and Melody, in Torrey. Melody turned up early with freshly made coconut balls for my journey, just as I got an email, *"Hi this is Hannah. Can I cycle with you today? Will you wait for me?"* Hannah is a twenty-six-year-old EMT/Fire-fighter from Colorado. She's cycling across the USA and had heard I was just in front of her, from Jerry, on his tricycle. *"Sure, I'll wait."* There was a big hill to climb, and having company for the first time in ages, would be great. We met at Subway, she with a lovely smile, and bouncing with youthful enthusiasm.

In 2013, Ju and I had driven up this hill. It seemed to go on forever. Cycling it was the same, but having company lightened the load considerably. We were passed several times by cycling teams training for the Tour of Utah which starts next week. They wouldn't move quite as fast if they had Fiona's load. But then, finally, we had a downhill. 70kph. Woohooo, and with lightening striking the hills on both sides of the road, now that's exciting. Into Boulder, we think. *"Have we missed Boulder?"* *"No Sir. This shop is Boulder."* Then we climb again, up on to the Hogsback Ridge, a very narrow road along a very exposed ridgeline, fantastic. Best, is that I know where there is a really nice campsite.

We meet Jason and his family at the campsite. He tells us some of the history of the Mormons, and about Pioneer Day. He is a cycling nut. Owns over twenty bicycles, many of them BMX. He is excited about the Olympics coming up, as am I.

Early next morning, Hannah and I head out. The views off the Hogsback are amazing, and it's downhill. We nearly collide with a bride. They are out getting early morning photographs of her in her bridal gown. She has just recently returned from an eighteen month mission in NZ. We get included in some photos. *"If you hurry, you might get to watch the Pioneer Day parade in Escalante."*

We don't hurry. It's getting hot, and it's all uphill, but we do get to Escalante to see the parade. It's interesting, but not stunning, and far too much candy thrown out to the kids, but all the locals seemed to enjoy the occasion.

Later, much later, we arrive in Tropic. We are both very tired. Let's try the Fire Brigade. No one home there, so I cross the road to ask a local if she knew how to contact the Chief. *"Why don't you just camp on our lawn? Need a shower? Want to share pizza?"* Once again, we experience an unexpected and amazing evening, with our hosts; a fantastic evening of learning and discussion, heralded by Pioneer Day fireworks. I learnt about the generosity and peace-loving nature of Mormons but was dumbstruck when Annette told me she carried a gun in her purse. Kirk, a retired Cowboy, Rancher, and volunteer Fire-fighter/EMT, told me that probably 90% of the local population carried concealed weapons. Love thy neighbour but be prepared to defend yourself. WOW.

And then Hannah and I started the real climb. Two days of up, up, up. We passed Red Canyon, an amazing mountain biking area, and had a short respite, but by just before dark we were shattered. A flat area under conifers was our resting spot. This area is really beautiful if you like open conifer forest, and then in the morning more up, to just below 10,000 feet, but no signage. It was TOUGH. The 20 miles (32kms) of downhill into Cedar City, almost made up for the climb. More important was a big feed, a new tyre for the trailer, laundry, and a rest. A couple of more days and we will be in Nevada.

DESERT BASINS

30th July 2016

Cedar City to Wah Wah Pass 140km
To Sacramento Pass 106km
To Robinson Pass 108km
To Eureka Nevada 103km
To Austin Nevada 114km

In Western Utah and Eastern Nevada there are a series of ridges running north/south between 6000 and 8000 feet, with huge basins, also running north/south, between them. Our route takes us across these ridges and basins, and it's amazing, tough, spectacular, huge, and hot, and there aren't too many people out here.

We have about eleven of these ridges to climb altogether, and so far, we've conquered six. Woohoo, we are over halfway. Each is different, but the toughest are those with long straight roads. Coming down off one ridge we can see the road disappearing across the valley. For 5 miles (8kms) we speed downhill at 35 mph (60 kph). For 5 miles (8) we fight along the flat into a head wind at 10mph (16 kph). Then for the next 5 miles (8kms) we grind uphill at 4 mph (7 kph). And there's so little in the valleys. One had a group of farm buildings nestled behind some trees, away off in the distance. Another had a 'fern' of sixty wind turbines. One basin had a lone horse. We see very few animals but are warned they are out there.

The biggest challenge, after the gruelling uphill, is having enough water. Between Hannah and I we are carrying over 20l of fluid, and we keep running out. We made it to a 'town' yesterday, with half a litre between us. The town consisted of a bunch of run-down houses, and a Post Office, which, fortunately, was open. The Post Mistress poured us a couple of litres each out of her gallon jar, which she brings from home each day. The PO has no running water. Then we got to hear the history of the town, and everyone who had lived there for the last thirty years. I think the Post Mistress needed someone to talk to.

We've made a sign. 'Water Please'. We strap it to the back of Hannah's bike. It works. People stop. A guy who has just been cycling the Divide route filled our bottles with glorious cold fresh water.

We are starting to cycle early, at first light, and trying to get to another small town by midday. If there is anywhere to do so, we buy a meal, then we find, if we can, a shady spot and rest, nap, snooze, for an hour or two, hoping that it will cool down. About 4pm, we cycle again, into the hills, trying to get a bit of altitude, where hopefully, it might be cooler to sleep. It's working so far.

We're still meeting locals. The school caretaker in one town had lots of advice: watch for deer on the way down from Sacramento Pass, and Elk after Austin Pass. The panel beaters in this area are making a fortune from vehicles messing with animals. He also told me he has for many years been a track and cross-country coach, using Arthur Lydiard's methods of training.

Some folk are really friendly and generous, but amazingly, some of the shop and cafe owners are pretty grumpy. They don't seem so happy that we have come to spend our money. Hmmmm. Sorry to put you out guys.

In Eureka we were invited to a party. The local school rock band was playing in the street, to welcome a bunch of Balloonists. They weren't too bad, especially the Beatles set, which had me singing, and swinging. (I'm missing my band time and can't wait to mix it with Test of Time again). We got chatting to one of the balloonists, and invited on a flight, but the next morning was a bit windy.

Hannah is a gem. Always has a smile. I haven't heard her complain once, and she has every right to, as the road is tough going. When a vehicle passes you, you can watch it shrink to a dot, and then disappear completely, and you know it hasn't gone around a corner, because you can see the road going straight, uphill, beyond where the vehicle disappears. Its tortuous, brain numbing, character testing stuff, and Hannah is passing with honours. I'm very lucky to have her along as company. Youth at its best (and she's pretty).

As for me: my clothes are so encrusted with salt from my sweating, that they could stand up alone. My lips are soooo very sore, from either wind burn or sunburn, even though I've been layering them with lip balm. The salt on chips stings them. My lips hurt when trying to bite into a sandwich. Damn. I have a huge blister in my groin, which makes it very uncomfortable to cycle. Don't even imagine how I'm going to solve that one, or who I'm going to enlist to help. My calves are so, so close to cramping up all day. I can feel them twinging at every pedal stroke. They wake me in the mornings when I stretch. Oowww. And that despite drinking lots of electrolyte. When I climb, my mouth gets absolutely desert dry. Not a drop of saliva. My tongue sticks to the roof of my mouth. I can't eat anything without drinking fluid at the same time. Maybe I'm drinking too much electrolyte? Damn. I'm feeling like an old crock.

But wait. Is Hannah finally flagging? I'm sure she's in granny gear and slowing. Damn. I can't really see. She's too far out in front.

We reckon nine more days cycling to San Francisco.

SURVEILLANCE?

2nd August 2016

Austin to Sand Springs Pass 130km
To Dayton 136km
To Kit Carson Pass California 85km

For the third time since being in the USA, while scrolling for Internet connections in very small towns, I've come up with Wi-Fi networks available: "FBI and/or DEA Surveillance". I haven't tried to connect using these networks. Who are they watching? Am I being watched? Have I been too long in the USA, or am I becoming paranoid?

Maybe if they heard about my latest plan, they'd be concerned. Seems to me there is a lot of empty land in Nevada, and it's dry. Well so is Syria. So now we convince the new President of the USA, that instead of spending money bombing Syrians, he/she spends it on relocating the Syrian Refugees to Nevada. With assistance from the USA government, I'm sure they could find water, build towns, and a mosque or two, and be very happy, away from all the other people bombing their homeland. Hmmmm. Wonder how that would go down with all the Trump voters in Nevada.

One of the biggest challenges of this whole trip has been eating, and it is no easier here in the USA. Normally you get to visit a Grocery Store only at the end of the day, when you're tired and hungry, a bad time. In the small stores the challenge is finding something that will replenish the calories you've burnt all day. Something wholesome, fresh, uncrushable, that won't spoil, and is not too heavy. In a big store, finding the right aisle, and then sorting the rubbish from the not so rubbish, is the challenge. Looks like cheese and crackers, with a tin of tuna, again tonight.

The best part of the whole trip is meeting people. In the last couple of days we've met: a couple of young fellahs making a dash for New York, with very light bikes; two lovely young Catalonian senoritas; a bunch of Harley riders from Switzerland; a kayaker turned cycle tourer heading east; Tom from Dot, Nevada, who is in charge of cycle safety, and shouted us breakfast; and a long haired blonde guy who has membership at Craigeburn Ski Area, and comes to NZ to ski and climb. Right now, he's training for a road race, the "508", on Sept 17th. Looks gruesome.

Then there was Kit. We meet him in a bottle store, in Mark Twain, while we were sipping Cold Raspberry Teas. He swaggers in with a pistol on his hip. I couldn't help but ask, "*Mr. I'm a naive NZ boy, and I'm fascinated with your gun.*" His reply, " *Cool isn't it.*" Me, "*A bit scary actually.*" He went on to explain the law in Nevada. "*If you can legally buy it, then you can carry it. Or you can get a licence to wear it concealed. In Australia, when they confiscated all the weapons, the crime rate soared. It's NOT going to happen here. We're protected.*" Hmmmm?

The terrain continues to be challenging. Today we crossed salt flats for miles, while being buzzed by *Top Gun* types from Fallon Navy Base; very scary, and very noisy.

We're heading towards the Californian border. Woohoo. Hannah is on day fifty-five of her crossing of the USA. I'm on day 800 of my circumnavigation of the globe, having cycled 29,000 miles (45,000km). Big woohooo.

AND JUST LIKE THAT

4th August 2016

Kit Carson Pass to Folsom 157km
To Yolo County 110km

We almost missed the sign at the border between Nevada and California, it was so insignificant. That's the problem with cycling the minor roads, and then almost immediately we began to climb, and it was hot, hot, hot. Well that really dampened the enthusiasm. We eventually got to an intersection, just in time to meet our first Californian on home soil. He was on a mountain bike with some luggage. *"Damn. Was your hill as friggen hot and steep as mine?"* He jumps off and bounces about. He's looking for a Frisbee golf course and seems to need his next fix, of something. He can't keep still. We give him directions, because we can, and head uphill some more.

It's a beautiful valley. Open Redwood forest, with huge rock features, but it's steep, there are roadworks, and it's hot, damn hot. We struggle. We stop many times for refreshments, and finally give up 6 miles (10km) before the summit, pitching the tent behind a screen of trees, 5m from the road. But it's an effective screen. Sometime later a young German cyclist bikes right past us. I give chase and stop him, and we chat. He's cycled up from Tahoe and wants to camp at the summit.

In the morning, a very chilly morning, where I'm contemplating digging out socks and gloves. The climb seems a lot easier, perhaps because the scenery is so stunning. Today, I'm stopping to take photos. We reach Kit Carson Pass, a tad over 8000 feet, our last climb. Well not quite. The German guy joins us on the downhill, and half a dozen grunty, unexpected climbs. Mostly the road is really great, but a couple of times, where they are doing roadworks, the judder bars, hidden in the shadows, gave us all big scares. Not fun at 65kph on a bicycle. We part ways with the German after 3000 feet descent. He's heading for Yosemite. We're heading for Folsom (Johnny Cash Prison). It's a fun downhill, but there's nowhere to camp. But amazingly, Hannah produced a Warmshowers Host, and we get to spend a delightful evening with Paul and Anne and eat scrumptious pasta. Thank you, thank you, and thank you.

The American River has a cycle way, and it was lovely - smooth, shaded, and no big hills, which made for a lovely 70 miles (100km) after yesterday's 100 miles (160km). Lots of cyclists showed a good deal of interest in our trip, and it was fun mixing it with others for a change. An hour or so cycling through orchards, and we decided we'd had enough for the day, and found a campground, with showers, for only $5.00, fantastic. A quiet afternoon, sitting in the shade. We figure this will be our last night on the road, so I dig out my emergency meal. It's sat in my trailer ninety days. One can beans, one can sweet corn, one can tuna, and one can chicken, ten tortillas. Yummy.

And then a day cruising, through lovely wooded valleys, with a few, quite a few, testing little hills, an hour on a ferry, some shoving through crowds of milling tourists at Fisherman's Wharf, and JUST LIKE THAT, we're standing below the Golden Gate Bridge, being splashed by the surf of the Pacific Ocean. WOW.

TRANSITION CALIFORNIA

11th August 2016

San Francisco,
Los Angeles,
San Diego.

As Hannah and I descended from the mountains, the first indication that we were in transition was the six-lane motorways, with thousands of cars speeding past our previously quiet cycle paths. We had a short respite while we cruised across the bay on a ferry, but when it berthed at Fisherman's Wharf, we were thrown into real life. Thousands of tourists were pushing their way past the shops, restaurants and street performers. We looked at each other with disbelief. "Oh, my goodness. Where have we ended up?" The crowds thinned a little as we headed towards the Golden Gate Bridge, but still there were hundreds of tourists on bicycles, heading along the trails towards the bridge. Not nearly as many actually cycled all the way to the bridge, and we hung out there for a while, soaking in our achievement, and enjoying the sanctuary away from the throngs. It was a weird feeling. I asked Hannah, *"What now?"* and we both laughed, with a shrug. Yep, so what do we do now? I remember seeing the same question asked amongst Pilgrims finishing the Camino de Santiago, in Spain. We decided our next move was to find accommodation.

On my map, I found some hostels, so we cycled back into the city. The best route turned right. Oh bother, it's uphill. No, it's not just up hill, it's the street you see in all the movies, where cars chase each other, and fly over the bumps. It's a series of very steep inclines, with short flat sections between. We are fully laden, and getting cheered by tourists, who are struggling to walk up the slopes. Leavenworth Street. We stopped to ask a cop how far we had to go. *"Only another three or four more ups. Man, you guys are tough."*

And then, the hostels are all full, and really expensive. We eventually get a very untidy room, that we're sharing with two others, for $65.00 each a night. *"How come you decided to come to the most expensive city in the USA, on the busiest weekend of the year?"* Apparently, there is some huge music festival happening.

We eat, we sort gear, and we buy tickets. Hannah is flying back to Colorado at 6am on Sunday. I'm going to LA by train, except San Francisco doesn't have a railway station, so the first five hours is in a bus, but I don't have to box up Fiona. I help Hannah load her stuff into a shuttle at 4am and go back to bed. I have the luxury of a 7am start and cycle the mile or so to the bus station.

Fiona and all my gear fit easily under the bus, and I meet a lovely young lady to chat to on board. The five hours whizz by, and then the five hours on the train are really scenic, so the trip was not nearly as arduous as it might have been. Folk on the train give me advice as how to get to Manhattan Beach. *"No, you should not even attempt to cycle there. Take the Metro. It's Sunday, it shouldn't be busy."* They forgot about the Dodgers game. I had to go on three different lines, negotiate several escalators, and find the special sections for bicycles. Trouble is, LA folk, and especially very happy, intoxicated Dodgers fans are not too polite. I missed two trains because I wasn't aggressive enough pushing Fiona on board. Oh well. Eventually, I made it to the end of the line, and Myles was there to meet me.

Myles is from Kaiapoi, making it big in LA. He and partner Brittany have offered to put me up for a couple of days: more amazingly generous folk. They live 800m from the sea at Manhattan Beach. Pretty special place, but it's also very busy with beautiful people. This definitely is not Iran. There is a lot of flesh being flashed, more than I've seen in a very long time, and everything is pretty expensive, even in the supermarket. Flash cars, beach cruiser bicycles, surfboards, skateboards, muscle bound bodies, beach volleyball, whistle blowing lifeguards, and more. Nope. It's definitely not Nevada either. But I'm not staying long. I'm very keen to get to San Diego.

Annie lives in San Diego, with husband Royer. I've known Annie for over thirty years. She's a Rotherham girl, with an amazing job in a local University Hospital. It's a long time since we've caught up, and the train ride, along a gorgeous coastline, is a small price to pay, to see her again. We bore Royer silly, reminiscing, catching up with what families and friends are up to, and just enjoying each other's company. Royer takes a day off to show me around. He's amazed that I stop to talk to so many people, and equally amazed that they actually let me talk to them. I said, *"That's what we do in Hanmer Springs, we talk."*

I'm very happy, but my journey is not over with another train journey to LA. Juliet arrives tomorrow. I'm very excited. We are flying to Oregon then cycling the last overseas section of my journey together, from Portland Oregon, along the west coast, back again to LA. Sharing it with such an amazing lady, it's going to be fantastic.

WITH MY LOVE

17th August 2016

Portland Oregon to Venonia 75km
To Astoria 104km
To Nehalem 85km

Yep. I'm excited. Ju arrives in the morning. Myles reckons she will take a couple of hours to get through Immigration, but Brittany reckons we should get there a bit earlier, perhaps ninety minutes after she lands. No problem to me. I hardly sleep. And then Ju rings forty-five minutes after she lands, *"I'm through. Where are you?"* Oooops. Luckily, it's only a twenty-minute drive from home. But then, Ju has told me Terminal 5, and we can't find her. Another loop and I spot her outside Terminal 2. Woohooo! Six months since I've seen her.

She's tired, but a breakfast revives her, followed by a walk to the beach, then it's a long snooze. That gives me time to finish packing Fiona for our flight to Portland. Thank you, Myles and Brittany, for your wonderful hospitality. You made Ju's arrival so easy.

I've joined Uber and have ordered an SUV for the early morning trip back to the airport. With two bikes and panniers it seemed the best idea, and in fact it works really well. Then the check in with South-western Airlines was really easy as well. Smooth travel. Ju has been in touch with Chris in Portland. *"Come and stay at my house. My brother has a Pizza place and sells craft beers."* Sounds great. He also suggests the MAX train, from the airport out to Hillsboro. So easy, and the train travellers in Portland are so polite compared with those in Los Angeles. Our fare is $5.00, and the ticket machine spits out fifteen dollar coins in change. I didn't even know the USA had dollar coins. My right pocket feels very heavy. We jump off the MAX and put our bikes together in the shade of some trees next to the platform, and cycle to Chris's house. So easy.

Chris takes us to his brother's pizza and beer place (pizza schmiza, I think), then shows us around Portland. There has been a huge cycling festival in the city today. There are bicycles everywhere. The whole city has a really cool vibe going on, but before we fall for it, we are warned that it rains seven months of the year. Oh well.

Chris has shown us a route out of the city, leading all the way to the coast, but before we leave I need to post our bike bags to LA, Ju needs to buy a sleeping mat, I need a new Sim card, we need to stock up with food, and most importantly, we have a coffee date with Anicka and Coradyn Dvorak. It's a bit of a rush, but we make it to coffee on time. So great to see Anicka and meet Coradyn. Perhaps next time will be in NZ. Then Ju gets lost, looking for REI. How could I lose her, when I've just found her???? My fault entirely. I should have known she had gone inside through the back door. Sorry my love.

Eventually we hit Chris's route. It's fantastic. There is very little traffic, scenic, and no hills, following a pretty river. A great way for Ju to get into the groove, and for the first time in a long while, I'm not chasing a deadline. My reason for cycling so fast is now cycling with me. I just have to get her to slow down. After 50 miles (80 km), we find a lovely spot near a lake to camp. Ju pretends she's really tired.

Day two is more beautiful scenery, with a little climbing, with once again very little traffic. It takes us to Astoria, the oldest settlement west of the Mississippi. This time Ju really is tired. She's cycled her first 60 miles (100km) day, and there is nowhere to camp. We find a Motel, and a Mexican restaurant. We are both smiling, me at the fantastic burrito, Ju at the huge margarita; me at having spent two whole days with my lovely wife, Ju at the hot shower, and comfortable bed, me at reaching the Pacific Coast again, and at Lisa Carrington winning a Gold Medal, Ju at the coffee machine in the corner, and a guaranteed coffee before cycling tomorrow.

Day three and we start south. But what's this? 'Road Closed'. Perhaps we will be able to sneak through. Nope. It's a 3 mile (5km) back track, but we find a nice breakfast spot, and meet a Korean cyclist, touring from the Arctic Circle to Patagonia. Hmmmm. Wasn't that my original plan? Yes, it was, but I'm really glad to be heading home with my gal. This coastal route is stunning. The weather is really good. Not too warm, and not wet, as it can be here. So far, we have been very lucky. Some of the towns are very busy, it's still holidays here, and at times the road is very busy, but mostly we have a good shoulder to ride on. We arrive at Nehalem State Park to our first Hiker/Biker campsite. The campsite is full with normal campers, but there are special sites for cyclists and hikers. We only pay $6.00, what a deal. Oh, how lucky am I? I'm doing something I love, and I'm sharing it with my love. Yep. I'm smiling.

BEACHES, HEADLANDS AND INLETS

20th August 2016

Nehalem SP to Cape Lookout SP 81km
To Devils Lake State Park 72km
To Beachside State Park 85km

Hiker/Biker campsites are cool. Two days now, we've turned up to a 'Campsite Full' sign and still been given a spot. Both days the site has been away from the noise and ruckus of all the families on holiday, the teenage parties, and drunken singing around campfires. Both nights we've been under tall trees, with the sound of the Pacific Ocean pounding ashore. Tonight, we even have an ocean view, and at a cost of $6.00 each. Fantastic value.

Now here's a funny story that may not get past my new live-in editor. We went to REI the other day so Ju could buy a new sleeping mat. Good price and a comfortable first night sleep resulted in thumbs up. But then Ju is trying to pack the mat up and was having great difficulty getting all the air out. "The valve was just in a blimmen stupid position. I'm taking this blimmen thing back." Night two unwrapping her partially inflated mat, "Oooops. There's another valve here, one for inflation, one for deflation. Lucky, I didn't find another REI and gone in ranting." Hehehe.

Another 'Road Closed' today, but we asked a Sheriff whether we could get through with our bikes. He gave us the nod, which meant we had virtually a clear road for 6 mile (10km), with no traffic, and it was stunning, even with the big climb halfway along. The views are great, the beaches beautiful. The weather great for cycling, although a little foggy in the morning, and I've got Juliet by my side. Happy days.

I'm continually surprised when we arrive at places. Almost always they are not how I imagined. Today, a town I expected to be a small fishing village was a big city, with all the usual fast food and outlet stores. Another town, which I expected to be a plush resort, turned out to be almost like a central Asian resort. Everything was scruffy and run down. USA towns always surprise me. They are not compact, with a central CBD like in NZ. Some have an older section that was once the core of the town, but most now have a strip of businesses on one of the main roads entering the town, all accessed by cars, and surrounded by huge car parks.

This route we are cycling is not what I expected either. I was looking forward to quiet, curving roads, along a beautiful coastline. We have got the beautiful coastline, but most of the route is on a busy main highway, 101, and being the middle of the summer holidays, it's really busy. Occasionally our route takes us on back roads, which are fantastic, but not often. Nevertheless, we are seeing some amazing views, and today we saw lots of whales.

But what's with the weather? Today it was foggy almost all day. Often, we couldn't even see the beach, and it was cold. And the ocean is really cold. So here are all these thousands of holiday makers, who have come to the coast to escape the heat of the inland valleys, and they can't even see the sea from the car park. Some were braving the cold winds and fog, and sitting on the beach, but most were in the towns and villages shopping, or queuing for food, which explains why we had such a long wait for very expensive, inferior quality, fish and chips. Every day a challenge.

This route is a very busy cycling route. In four days, we've met three individual guys cycling from Alaska to Patagonia, a couple of USA guys touring locally, two English guys heading from Vancouver to Mexico, and seen numerous cyclists going north (but none of them stop to chat. Unheard of on other routes). Some of the younger ones are doing big mileage. But then, I suppose, just weeks ago I was the same. They have a target and are aiming for it. My focus has changed. I'm on holiday with the lovely Juliet. We have thirty-five days to cover what's advertised as a twenty-five-day route. We are in chill mode and loving it.

CHARACTERS ON THE COAST

25th August 2016

Beachside State Park to Florence 51km
To Sunset Beach State Park 100km
To Humbug Mt State Park 98km
To Harris Beach State Park 87km
To Crescent City California 50km

It seems that this Oregon Coastline has a few similarities to New Zealand's West Coast. In particular, we are meeting several interesting characters.

At our first Biker/Hiker site we met a local guy, cycling the coast for the tenth or twelve time. He had all the answers, even though we hadn't asked any questions. But he didn't want to ruin the movie for us, so didn't tell us much anyway. He told us stories of sitting out storms of several days, in some of the campsites, of leaving early in the morning, then hiding a few miles from the campsite, and watching the young European cyclists racing to try and catch and pass him, and of accompanying pretty young female cyclists from Japan, France and Australia. We heard his stories for two nights, as he 'raced' us to the second Hiker/Biker site.

Then there was Jess, a young teacher from Vancouver Island. She was surfing the coast over her summer holiday, sleeping in her car at the side of the road, following steep trails down to isolated beaches to surf mean breaks, and struggling in and out of her 6ml wetsuit to keep warm in the freezing water. She was having a ball.

What about the Santa/Gandalf/JC look alike at Hiker/Biker campsite three? He scurried over to Ju as we arrived and led her through the trees to show her a secluded, beach front camping spot, which we rejected, then he kept his distance, for a while. Next, he started bringing firewood on to our site, but when we tried to engage him in conversation, he slunk away. He sat and watched us from a distance, occasionally waving if we looked his way. Later still, he came and tried to light our fire, but still no conversation. At dusk, he invited me to warm myself by his fire. Turns out he's an author, and poet. His first question to me was, *"So how is it in NZ, living with those jade carving, rugby mad Maori?"* We had a very interesting conversation, perhaps bordering on Christian indoctrination, but certainly very knowledgeable about USA politics, foreign policies, and very opposed to the gun laws. In the morning, as we were leaving, my new friend ran after us, in his very short, calf length bell bottom trousers, and handed me a list, written on a brown paper bag, of the restaurants and campsites we would see over the next few days. Before I could thank him, he was heading back to his hidey hole, conversation over.

The Laundromat lady: I walked in on her conversation with Ju, when Ju was explaining that NZ was having winter right now. *"Wow, that's weird. Sort of like on the east coast of the USA. You know, they never see the sun set into the ocean."* She couldn't grasp that in NZ it was warm in the north, and cold in the south. *"Can you drive off your island?"* We chatted about weights and measures. *"You guys must be mathematical geniuses, working out all those litres and stuff."* *"Do you have dollars? What about hours, minutes and seconds?"* I'm pretty sure she was voting for Mr Trump.

And then the weather has character of its own. It's high summer and we are wearing four layers of clothes. Yesterday we had a fierce tail wind, great for pushing us along, but stop and it's freezing, and the sea fog? I reckon we've only been able to see 50% of the coast; the rest has been lost in the fog. It's so nice heading inland and finding the sunshine.

What about the animals along this coast? There are lots of whales out and about, when we can see the ocean and the raccoons and skunks prowl through the campsites at night. One guy caught a raccoon hauling his pack away. Hehehe. And then there's the Kiwi couple. He is all starry-eyed and smiling like the Cheshire Cat. How could he not be? He loves having his wife cycling with him; so lucky.

CYCLING AMONGST THE GIANTS

28th August 2016

Crescent City to Prairie Creek SP 61km
To Eureka 87km
To Humboldt Redwood SP 100km

I love the Redwoods in Hanmer Springs. But just imagine 2000 plus acres of them, with a two lane, almost traffic less road weaving between these gigantic trees. That's what Juliet and I are experiencing right now. It's awesome.

We've worked to get here though. Inland from here it's hot at the moment. This heat draws in the cold air from the ocean, which brings with its Sea fog. That's great for the Redwoods but makes everything else pretty damp and cold. Luckily, I didn't send all my warm gear home. We are often wearing two, three, and sometimes four layers of clothes, and this is summer? But oh, so worth it.

There are a lot of cyclists on this route. I'm sure I've seen more here the whole of the USA. The good thing is, you get to meet them several times, as they are cycling the same route. The German lad, Uli, we met in Astoria caught up with us the other day, and we cycled together. He's heading to South America and is in no hurry as he wants to cycle through Death Valley. He hopes, that if he takes his time, by the time he gets there, it may have cooled down a little. He camped with us last night. Ju cooked some very horrible, store bought, macaroni cheese. She gave me the first batch, which I ate. Uli arrived back just after I finished eating, and as Ju started preparing the second batch. She served it up, and ate in front of us. Uli, "*Is this punishment for being away two years? Your wife cooks and then eats all the food, and doesn't share?*" Me, "*Yep. But I suppose I deserve it really.*" Uli, "*Hmmmm. You Kiwis have strange ways.*" We ate breakfast with Uli at a restaurant, and then he went to a supermarket, and we haven't seen him since. Perhaps tomorrow.

We met a guy skateboarding from Seattle to LA. It was great chatting to him, sharing stories. He skates over 100 miles (160km) a day, thirteen hours. He told me his feet are killing him, as he has to ride the back roads. A skateboarder is considered a pedestrian and isn't allowed on the nice smooth 101 highway. His mother is following him, not on a skateboard, with all his gear, food, water, and I hope spare shoes.

Another couple, newly retired, are making a lap of the USA. They expect to take a couple of years, as they may return home to Seattle when the seasons change. They're loving the relaxed pace that retirement allows. Their first cycling trip was some years ago, when they took their sons, twelve and fourteen years, to Disneyland, from Seattle, on bicycles.

A group of Quebecois are also cycling in parallel with us. It's really fun catching up with them in the evenings, exchanging stories of our day. It makes such a huge change from the long lonesome days I've experienced at times over the last couple of years. One thing that really amuses me is the talk of the huge climbs on this route. I bite my tongue, as they tell of how they conquered, or not, these mountains. 1200 foot doesn't really feel like a climb, compared with the 10,000- and 11,000-foot passes Hannah and I climbed to get to California. But hey; it's fantastic to see so many out here challenging themselves.

Someone in New York has my Credit Card number. They are buying up large, taxis, meals, online purchases. The good old BNZ noticed the irregularities, and knowing we were in California, and not New York, cancelled the card, which is fantastic, except, now we have no credit card. We got a message to ring the BNZ collect, but do you think we could get a USA company to make a collect call. I am so impressed with my amazing wife. She made seven very long telephone calls, to seven different people, and didn't lose her cool once, on the phone. Eventually she just rang direct to the BNZ to try and sort something out. Hmmmm, yet another challenge. We need new cards. They will send them to us. What's our address? They will take three weeks. Well that's not going to work. Hopefully Ju's Debit Card will suffice, and the $500 cash I have in my pocket will last the thirty days until we fly home. I love a good challenge, and they keep coming.

And the giant Redwoods will continue tomorrow. Such amazing scenery, and sharing it with such an amazing lady, makes this part of my journey one of the very best experiences of the last two years. How come I'm so lucky?

FALLING THROUGH THE GAPS

31st August 2016

Humboldt Redwood to Standish Hickey 78km
To Russian Gulch SP 96km
To Gualala SP 88km

The other day we arranged to stay with Kate, a Warmshowers host. It turned out that we were sleeping in a church hall, and on the one night a month that the church fed the needy of the town. We got to help prepare, serve and clean up, as well as share the meal. No talk of religion, just a ring of people singing the 'Johnny Appleseed Song' before eating. Perhaps thirty or forty people turned up for the meal.

Some used the church hall shower to clean up before eating. Most were very polite. All ate at least two helpings. There were street people, families, a few Native Americans, several teenagers, a couple of handicapped, and five of us cycle tourers. We were told that sometimes there can be up to eighty people queuing for the meal. In Portland we saw many homeless and street people. We were told that many have been bused by authorities, up to Portland from California, because Portland looks after their needy. But the Portland people are not happy. Public parks, footpaths and reserves are all being swamped by tents, tarpaulins and shelters. 'Regular' residents are being hassled by these 'transients'.

As we cycle through the amazingly scenic 'Avenue of the Giants', every so often we pass through a small town. It seems these towns are rife with transients; scruffy, unwashed, smelly, beggars, with all their belongings in dirty backpacks, or in supermarket trolleys, and many smoking pot. As we cycle south, into warmer areas, we see more and more of these people, living under bushes on the beaches, and sleeping in parks. But how can this be? Isn't the USA one of the wealthiest nations in the world? I've asked several people, and the most common replies are: "they've just slipped through the gaps" or "they've decided it's easier to live like this, than struggle to pay mortgages, power and utility bills, insurance, and taxes. They've opted out of normal society and are living in a world where they've only got two problems - where is my next feed coming from, and where will I sleep tonight?"

Now I can relate to those two 'problems', having asked the same question myself every day for the last two years, but I certainly do not believe I'm in the same category as these folks. Many seem to have either given up all hope, or are beyond caring about the future, what they look like, how they appear to others, how much they smell, or what their living conditions are. For me the two scariest things are that there are so many of these people, and that my country is following this trend.

That's not to say that the countryside isn't amazingly beautiful. We climbed out of the Redwoods and over the highest hill on this route. We had heard of exhausted cyclists, and piles of discarded panniers. We saw neither. Instead we climbed up a beautiful road, through luscious forest, and descended through glorious windy smooth corners, where I had to brake for 10, 15, 20, 25, and 30mph corners. Oh what amazing fun. And, to top it off, when we descended from the second, lower pass, we found blue skies over a clear ocean, with whales breaching, and seals barking; glorious. The only hazard of the whole climb and descent was having enough luck to be able to dodge the logging trucks, racing each other up and down the slopes.

A guy introduced himself. He seemed to be in his early 50s. He was a retired Fire Commander. He had honeymooned in NZ, but was now home-schooling his two boys, about eight to ten years old. He had loved NZ and was keen to take his boys to visit.

We met another guy. He had just been diving, trying to spear fish. He hadn't been too successful, but he had scored himself an abalone (pāua). This abalone was huge. As big as a rugby ball. Apparently, they are allowed a maximum of three a day, but I'm unsure how you'd eat that much.

I spoke to a guy from Hawaii. He was travelling with his family south, having just competed in a SUP (stand up paddle board) race, on the Columbia River. He told me he was friends with the fastest female SUP rider in the world, Annabel Anderson, from Wanaka. Who knew? Well maybe some of my Wanaka friends did.

Another guy told us he had lived on his bike, travelling up and down this coast for ten years. Instead of front panniers, he had a large white bucket strapped to one side, and a guitar strapped to the other. He has friends everywhere, and stops with them, helping with odd jobs, before he moves on. He had lots of helpful hints about the weather, places to stay, and places to eat.

Then we camped with a young couple of first-time cycle tourers, from out East, who now live in Seattle. This coastal route is not only spectacularly scenic; it's also the most social cycling and camping I've experienced in over two years. And when the store at Elk has fresh baked chocolate chip cookies, and ice-cold Bundaberg Ginger Beers. You've gotta love it.

END OF THE SUMMERTIME

3rd September 2016

Gualala SP to Bodega Dunes SP 84km
To Samuel P Taylor SP 71km
To San Francisco 69km

We've been invited to join a family for a BBQ dinner. Lots of hamburgers, fresh vegetables, and interesting chat. The family is a mixture; a couple of Americans, two South African brothers, and a couple of Latino women. One brother had lots to say about Aussie Rugby, some of it not complimentary. The Americans were into Stand-up Paddle boards, and the Latinos into family and children. They are enjoying the last week of the summer holidays, before the influx which happens over the last weekend. I've been cycling in the USA since just before summer, Memorial Day Weekend, until just after Labour Day Weekend. It certainly has not been what I would call a typical summer, with the rain and cold of the East Coast, the intense heat of the South, the dry of the central deserts, and the fog of the NW. Perhaps Southern California will still be warm, sunny, and dry and the water might even be a swimmable temperature.

We continue to meet amazing people. Joel, a nurse from Portland, is cycling to Mexico with his poodle, Roxy. Roxy is pretty cute. She sits in an adapted bag on the rear of the bike, watching everything.

Neil and Ali are from Brisbane. I don't know why, but whenever I meet Aussies while touring, we seem to very easily drift into conversation. It's really nice. They are mixing cycling with occasional spurts of miles in Rental Cars. This gives them the opportunity to cover more ground and visit areas of particular interest. They have got a small problem, however. Their USA Visa started when they first touched down in the USA, even though they were just transiting to Canada. This means that their exit flight, from the USA is about a week after their visa expires. Reminds me of a similar situation Ju and I had in 1995.

We cycled into a small town looking for a snack. The obvious place was where all the cyclists were. The Santa Rosa Cycling Club was out for its Friday ride. The club has over 400 members and has five organised rides a week and we just happened to meet them all at one of their favourite watering holes. Some were very interested in our adventure, but others quite scathing. "Oh yeah. You've ridden from NZ. How'd you cycle across all that water?" Another offered us beds just out of San Francisco if our other arrangements fell through.

We were cycling through some beautiful country, in warm sunshine, mainly off busy roads. But as we close in on San Francisco, a fog begins to descend. We are getting close to the Golden Gate Bridge, the traffic is getting thicker, and now there are hundreds of tourists on bicycles, descending from the bridge. Screeching brakes, chaos, traffic congestion. It's very obvious that a very high percentage of these 'cyclists' have never been on a bicycle before, nor will they be cycling back uphill towards the bridge.

It's a steep climb, but we successfully dodge the mayhem. It's very windy on the bridge, but not completely fogged in, and a pretty cool experience, despite all the other riders, one I'm glad I saved to share with Ju. The foreshore of San Francisco was pretty crazy as well, but we had a mission; navigate to our Warmshowers host, before his mid-afternoon appointment. I had learnt about the steepness of the streets here when Hannah and I had tackled Leavenworth Street, but it seems whatever your plans, steep streets pop up in front of you. Today our route encountered stairs. Bother. The detours hit steep, very steep, uphills. Ju was muttering.

We managed to get to our hosts' before his appointment. Yeeha. And then we spent two very relaxed days exploring San Francisco, The Presidio, Fisherman's Wharf, and Golden Gate Park. The crowds at Fisherman's Wharf were crazy, being the last weekend of the holidays. The skaters and drum circles in the park were amazing. The second day included REI, Ju's favourite shop in the world, and a return to the Park on our bikes. But the biggest challenge and achievement was mastering the public bus system. Woohoo. And to top it off we were 'blessed' by a couple of African American women, who had both seen God, and were also 'blessed'. Thanks Sisters. Ju and I truly are 'blessed' and are really enjoying this time together.

YELLOW BIKE

7th September 2016

San Francisco to Halfmoon Bay 56km
To New Brighton SP 98km

Our host in San Francisco, runs a not-for-profit bicycle repair workshop. It's situated in the Tenderloin, a notorious area of San Francisco, known for unemployment, drugs, street people, and the sex trade. Yellow Bike accepts donations of old bicycles. A volunteer who is a qualified bike mechanic gives the bike a once over to see whether the bike is repairable. Then a local, unqualified mechanic, keen to learn the trade is set free with tools and helped to either repair the bike or dismantle it for parts. The parts are used for spares. The repaired bike is sold, at a very cheap price, to the repairer, or some other local in need of transport. Great outcomes: new skills being taught, cheap bikes being made available, work being offered to street people. Does anything like this happen in NZ?

It's Yellow Jacket season. Yellow Jackets are like wasps, and we've encounter them a few times lately. On the cool mornings they seem to be really drowsy, and that's when I've run into them. The other morning, I was stung three times. Damn, they hurt, and for several days after the sting, there is pain and itchiness. Another experience, like dog bites, that I could have done without.

Marijuana isn't meant to be legal in California, except for medicinal purposes. There must be a lot of very sick people here. I'm sure I've got High from secondary inhaling in the parks of San Francisco. I know San Francisco has a reputation to up hold, and we did visit Hippie Hill, but it seems as everyone in the park was high, or heading that way, especially near the Drum Circle, and at the Skating Park. If I didn't know better, I'd think California was going to 'pot'.

We thought we'd seen it all, but today, cruising into Santa Cruz, we definitely saw it all, as we cycled past a nudist beach. I nearly fell off my bike, trying to cover Juliet's eyes. There are some things a young lady shouldn't see.

Ju and I have slowed down. We've got a bit of time before we need to be in LA, and there is a lot to see along this coast, so a day of 30 miles (50km) seemed appropriate. We were rewarded with cool tracks off the main route, including dirt tracks over a peninsula, with awesome views, and some time watching dolphins frolicking in the surf. This morning we watched a huge flock of sea birds diving for fish just offshore. I'm pretty sure the fish had been rounded up by the dolphins, and the clouds of birds were having a feeding frenzy. While we watched the birds, cute little rabbits were running around us, until a Red-tailed Eagle swooped down and took one for a flight, before eating his breakfast. Nature is amazing. Ju wants to try a bit of surfing here in Santa Cruz, so maybe we will do that in the next few days as well.

STRAWBERRY FIELDS

13th September 2016

New Brighton SP to Monterey Veterans Park 70km
To Limekiln SP 92km
To Hearst San Simeon SP 72km
To San Luis Obispo 74km

We were told the ride towards Mexico was going to be boring, but we found it anything but boring. We rode for hours through fields of strawberries, artichokes, peppers and other indistinguishable vegetables, all being harvested by huge numbers of Mexican workers. You have to wonder how many are legal. Then we dodged heavy traffic for an hour on a main highway, before slipping onto a cycle path that took us into Monterey. And en route we met, as usual, some fascinating people, like the airline pilot who twenty-five years ago had cycled across the USA, and was really excited to meet us, and the recently retired cop, married to an ER nurse, who was just thankful that he had survived his twenty-five years' service. No, it wasn't boring, and neither was the previous evening.

As we arrived in New Brighton, so did the fog. It got really cold. The next morning wasn't too different, but Ju was keen to hang out to see if it warmed up, so she could go surfing. It didn't. But that meant we needed to stay at the campsite two nights. Officially you can only stay one night. No problem said two different park staff. Just self-register. Oooops. Just on dark the Hiker/Biker site is visited by a Park Ranger. She has a gun on one hip, a Tazer on the other, a big badge and an attitude. Everyone on the campsite got nailed. The English didn't have their receipts taped to their bikes. The Swiss family had only filled out one form instead of four. The Americans only had one form, and we had already stayed a night. No amount of arguing (I did try), was going to get us anywhere except, "I could cite you, arrest you," Both hands on weapons. Taser and gun. We had to move to another site, in the dark, and pay an extra $25. Poor Park Ranger. I hope she felt better after venting her frustration on all us vulnerable and innocent tourists.

The following night was almost as exciting. A woman camping on the Hiker/Biker site, who seemed a little under the weather, drug or alcohol induced, was shipped out in the middle of the night by Police, Ambulance, Fire Brigade and Park Rangers. They even packed up her tent into a rubbish bag and took that away. Meanwhile, another camper, who had also been acting a little strangely during the afternoon, grunted, groaned and moaned all night, very loudly, keeping everyone, except me, awake. Apparently, he was a 'vet' with Post Combat Stress Syndrome. Knowing that didn't help everyone else sleep though.

Monterey was very nice. We watched a parade, the Italian, Catholic Community Celebrations, and then we went for a cruise out along the coast and onto 17 Mile Rd, where we saw lots of gated communities, and very fancy houses, surrounded by plush Golf Courses. Apparently, these homes (holiday homes, which are used two weeks a year), are owned by the 1%. Seems a little weird seeing so much wealth on one side of the hill, and so many homeless, hopeless cases on the other side of the hill, but this is America, where we are told it really is survival of the fittest (read richest).

We are meeting fascinating people. Like Jessie, a onetime drummer, and song writer, in a band sponsored by Van Halen, who after touring the USA for several years, became a councillor in a school for under privileged kids. He and his mother auditioned and got parts in a travelling Jesus Christ Superstar cast. He told us some amazing stories. And, a young couple, from South Dakota, on their first cycle tour. We've enjoyed their company several nights, and today even cycled with them for several hours. Touring this coast is very social.

And did I say it was spectacular? We spent the last two days cycling the coast near Big Sur. Stunning, and with the added excitement of huge bush fires, that have burnt right down to the road edge, closed camp sites and parks, and water restrictions. We watched a helicopter make several trips to a bay below the cliffs, to fill its monsoon bucket. And the animals? The last couple of days we've seen Sea Otters, Elephant Seals, Orcas, and Humpback Whales. The only negative, other than the grumpy Park Ranger, has been the amount of traffic, especially on the Sunday.

And now we only have two weeks before we fly back to NZ. Ju is excited, as today she passed 600 miles (1000km) on her bike, and we have at least another 300 miles (500km) to go. She feels like a 'real cycle tourer'. I'm not as excited. I've got very mixed feelings. I'm very keen to be home, but I'm not sure I'm as keen for this adventure to end. I'm really glad she's here to hold my hand these last few days.

SUNSHINE AND BIKINIS
16th September 2016

San Luis Obispo to Lompoc 102km
To El Capitan Beach SP 56km
To Carpentaria 62km

Yesterday we cycled out from beneath the cloud, away from the fog, and for the first time in a while, cycled in sunshine. California, up until now, certainly has not been as you see it in the movies, sunshine, bikinis and beach volleyball. It's been cold, often foggy, and windy. But suddenly that has changed. I saw my first bikini clad beach girl today. The sea has changed colour, from a cold grey green, to a clear blue, with startling white surf, and people are no longer wearing puffer jackets. The question is, will this strange phenomenon continue? We hope so.

Last night we treated ourselves to a Motel; hot showers, recharged electrics, good Wi-Fi, and two Mexican meals, and a long comfortable sleep without snorting raccoons looking for our food cache. It's got to be worth a few extra dollars.

We have cycled through an area heavy with 'Grannie' towns, RV Parks, and mobile homes. It seems the climate in this area suits the pensioners. Lots of well-manicured, neat and tidy mobile home parks, and RV Parks, and cafeterias filled with older folk. That doesn't mean they've all slowed down. There are plenty of grey-haired surfers, male and female, cyclists, joggers and walkers, and the golf courses we pass are pretty busy for mid-week.

It's getting warmer. Ju went for her first swim yesterday, and I saw my second bikini. This one was a lovely, two-piece, day glow pink. The wearer had long silky, blonde hair, a wonderfully sculptured body, and an Adams apple twice the size of his boobs. Hmmmm.

Yet another ideal of California was shattered yesterday. A group of families were on the beach. I was told they had hired a female lifeguard to watch over the swimmers. In my shallow, naive, TV and movie corrupted, male mind, I immediately thought, Pamela Anderson. Shattered. 5'2" tall and 5'2" round, wearing tight red cycle shorts, with a foghorn voice and the attitude of a Rottweiler. The kids were too scared to go in too deep, in case she came to rescue them. Job done. Imagine all the dads getting out of their depth, if Pamela was the lifeguard.

We cycled through Santa Barbara. It was all I'd expected. Very wealthy, small boutique stores, cafes and bars, with expensive cars sitting outside. Most people living in gated, locked communities, protecting themselves from the other half, those sleeping in parks, under bushes and on the beaches, with all their possessions in a stolen supermarket trolley. The very obvious difference between the haves and the have-nots keeps slapping me in the face.

We are just out of Los Angeles. We are meeting new cyclists and catching up with old acquaintances. It's still a lot of fun exchanging stories, plans and advice. I'm a little uncomfortable with being regarded as the expert, the most experienced. I still feel as if I'm learning every day. I'm still loving being on my bike. I love sharing this adventure with Juliet. (Last night she reached her arm over me in the tent. *Cool*, I thought—a cuddle. Nope. She was measuring how much room I had on my side of the tent.) It seems surreal to think that I have cycled around the globe, and equally surreal that in a few days it will all be over.

SEVEN DAYS TILL MARMITE

19th September 2016

Carpentaria to Leo Carrillo SP 82km
To Silverlake Los Angeles 67km

It was a very special moment cycling into LA, along the beaches. The end of this journey feels really close now; although we are still planning the two days' cycling down to see Annie and Royer in San Diego. For some of our cycling buddies the end couldn't come soon enough, but for me, it has almost arrived too quickly.

The cyclists all seemed to have regrouped. Couples from Quebec, England, South Dakota, and Ju and I shared the last Hiker/Biker site before LA, along with Dave - a transient - thinking of running for President. (He certainly had the ideas). In many ways it was a sad departure in the morning. We've shared many kilometres together, a few meals, and, for Ju, the odd beer, margarita, and wine.

But it's not only the cyclists we will miss. We met a lovely group of folk at a campsite the other night, on their annual church camp. We joined them for breakfast, and were invited, but declined supper. We also declined the multitude of invites to join their gatherings. I know. Incredibly shallow and unadventurous of us. But I had important stuff to do, like visit Marty the barber, and buy new reading material.

This area of the Pacific Coast has lots of military bases. Some you can cycle through, as long as you don't step off the road. Others you need to circumnavigate, following high, uncrossable fences. They do all have a commonality, young testosterone filled people driving 'hot' vehicles, loudly and fast, and lots of young families, many of them Hispanic. It seems the military must be a good option for new Americans.

One of the bases had a collection of missiles and strike aircraft on display Just outside the main gate. For me, this was a little disconcerting. Here, folks, are where your millions in taxpayer dollars, are being converted to weapons of mass destruction.

Another disconcerting point was that each weapon had its name written on it. Is that so those at the receiving end of a missile strike can recognise the type of weapon by which they've been obliterated? Still, we weren't the only tourists to stop and take photos, although unlike many of the others wandering through the exhibit, my thoughts were not of admiration.

The number of homeless and destitute we see still astounds me. Venice Beach, once a wholesome, if weird, tourist attraction, is now crowded with these 'forgotten' people. We hear stories of people with mental illnesses, and other medical problems, like cancer, whose insurance policies were not large enough to cover medical costs, and have sold everything to pay massive bills, and have been left with nothing. These are the people we see, reduced to sleeping in the open, and begging for food. It certainly says a lot about the social security benefits of NZ, even though some are slipping through there as well. Very sad.

We are being hosted by Amanda, a former client of mine, whom I guided around the North Island in 2002. That was her first ever hiking experience. Now she guides trips in the hills and mountains around LA for local Sierra Club members. She attributes her love for hiking and the outdoors to the wonderful guide she had in NZ. Hmmmm. Have to watch out for that trend. We don't want too many people crowding the outdoors we love.

It was an adventure getting to Amanda's. We decided to leave the bicycles at Manhattan Beach and catch the Metro. As usual, I underestimated the distance we had to walk to the first Metro Station, as all good guides do. We were only carrying one pannier each, but they got heavy quick. Panniers on a bike appear to be much lighter. Still, Ju didn't grumble (much), and the adventure navigating the several train changes, and the crowds, enriched our experience. The amazing Mexican meal, with Amanda, and the margarita, although smaller than those up the coast, helped lessen the pain of my miscalculations. And now we are chill axing, before our final two days cycling in the USA. (Being home is soooo close).

LAST DAYS

24th September 2016

Silverlake LA to Laguna Beach 88km
To San Elijo SP 93km
To Mexican Border San Diego 101km

Cycle touring is addictive. I'm unsure how I will cope with ordinary life once
I get back to Hanmer Springs and NZ. Every single day has its challenge.
Every single day has its encounters. Every single day you see something new,
something that amazes, something with a Wow factor, and these last few
days in the USA, that some cyclists write off as "boring urban cycling" have
not failed to fulfil all of the above. Let's see. What did we encounter?

The guy on the Harley, with his tiny dog sitting on the gas tank, wearing a
helmet, goggles and a leather jacket.

Two elderly gents zooming past us on Fat Bikes. How did that happen? Damn,
they're E bikes.

Navigating through suburban Los Angeles. Cycling through areas you've heard
of in movies, novels, TV programmes, like Laguna Beach, Newport Beach, San
Clemente, Del Mar, La Jolla.

Cycling along the concrete riverbanks of LA, those ones you've seen in dozens
of movie car chases.

Stopping to watch the multitude of surfers fighting for a position on the many
surf breaks.

Skate boarders, city cruisers, skaters, tourists, surfers, families, swimmers,
artists, walking the beachside pavements.

Experiencing the exhilaration of conquering yet another hill, photographing
the amazing view, and then hurtling down the oh so smooth downhills.

Cycling through a military base, and having to produce ID, then stopping for a
smoothie at the MacDonald's that is part of the large mall on the base.

Being offered help several times with directions from strangers. Being joined
by a local cyclist, who guided us through back streets, and onto a ferry,
crossing to Balboa Island, who didn't stop talking for 6 miles (10km), even to
ask what our names were.

Meeting a group of Sierra Club members—including a young lady who had just finished cycling across Canada—and sharing stories.

Meeting a couple of Pilipino American cyclists repairing a puncture, and then meeting the lady again the next day, with a group of her training buddies.

Seals, swimming with body surfers.

The *Queen Mary*. Lighthouses. Aircraft Carriers. Lots of helicopters (Ju's favourite), including the fixed wing craft that rotates its propellers up and down, depending on whether it wants to land, or go forward. Sunsets.

Spending another pleasant evening with Andrew and Diana from South Dakota.

Oh, and arriving within spitting distance of the Mexico border, then rushing back to Central San Diego, so as we could catch a ferry, and arrive at Annie's before dark, only to have Ju get a puncture.

Yep, I'm addicted. Not sure how the withdrawal will be, but now it's a train back to LA, and a long flight. I will worry about coping when I get home.

WHAT'S NEXT?

25th September 2016

San Diego to Los Angeles (by train)

I love to challenge myself. In the USA I cycled down the East Coast, across the South, and down the West Coast, 6,500 miles (10,300km). I cycled over high passes, through hot, very hot, deserts, and across very hot wet swampy areas. And just for fun, I decided to try and get a photograph of licence plates from all fifty states. On the penultimate day of cycling in the USA, I photographed number fifty, Hawai'i. Woohooo.

So now, I've only got 65 miles (140km) of cycling to accomplish, before I can truly lay this current challenge to rest. Cycling from Christchurch to Hanmer Springs will complete my circuit of the globe. I'm pretty excited about that, about being home, about seeing my family, reconnecting with friends, and the challenge of readjusting to what is regarded as 'normal' life. I will still need challenges, and adventures, but what will they be?

I suggested to Juliet that my next challenge should involve doing something that she enjoyed. Perhaps I should learn to surf. I reasoned that I probably need to spend three months over on the Gold Coast, learning in warm water, to be good enough to share the surfing experience with her. This suggestion did not go down too well. Guess I'm not spending three months on the Gold Coast.

I do want to convert my cycling fitness to a more rounded fitness. The couple of times I've tried running in the last couple of years have resulted in some very sore muscle groups. So that's going to be a challenge. One that will start very, very slowly. Anyone want to join me?

I do want to continue cycling. As I write, buddy Mike is rebuilding my Surly Karate Monkey so as I can mountain bike as soon as I get home. Yeeha. And there are a few places I would love to cycle tour, but not alone. Who wants to join me in NW India, Northern Vietnam, China and Northern Thailand, riding The Divide, Patagonia, on the Old Ghost Road?

Hiking NZ is running a hiking trip into the mountains of Peru next year. That sounds fun. And a challenge. Anyone interested?

But what about work, I hear you ask? I'm really excited about the prospect of returning to guiding and teaching first aid. I bring home with me new ideas for events in Hanmer Springs, ideas for a new business (or two, or three), new ideas of ways to be involved with, and challenge the Hanmer Springs community. Yep, I reckon I will be pretty busy, and sufficiently challenged work wise. Hopefully I might even make enough money to be able to eat.

I'm really looking forward to spending time with Juliet, my children and grandchildren, and my friends. I'm expecting many visitors, from all over the world, and want to repay the hospitality and kindness they shared with me as I cycled through their life. Oh yes, and maybe, just maybe, if I can find someone to help and advise me - a book. Now that really is a daunting challenge. It makes cycling through San Diego, catching trains with bikes, riding the LA Metro, and shuttle buses, then cycling through LA traffic to find our hotel, pale into insignificance. But I've only got 65 miles (140km) to cycle, and I will have cycled 30,000 miles (49,700km), around the world, through forty-one countries and nineteen states. I'm pretty chuffed with that, and it sets me up to be able to scoff at writing a book. How hard can that be?

THE HOMECOMING (PIES, BELGIUM BISCUITS, AND UNLIMITED MARMITE)

3rd October 2016

Los Angeles to Auckland 10,470km
To Christchurch 1,076km
To Hurunui 95km
To Hanmer Springs 55km

A day and a half in a Motel 6 in Los Angeles, breaking our bikes down into our Ground Effect bike bags, making sure that everything was clean enough to get through NZ customs (I even put on brand new tyres, since the old ones were practically bald) and our two bags per person were under the allowable 50lbs (23kgs), and not only did the check-in lady NOT bother weighing our bags, but the customs man in Auckland didn't even bother to open them to check whether everything was clean. We must look just soooo innocent.

I was nervous getting on the flight. I'm not afraid of flying, but this flight was taking me home. Did I really want to go home? What type of reception would I get? What am I going to do, if I'm not cycling through some exotic country? So many questions. So many unknowns. Hmmmm. So similar to every morning for the last 863 days, what am I going to eat? Where will I find food? Where am I going to sleep? What will I see and who will I meet today? Relax, I say to myself. Everything will be okay, and even if it's not okay we can make it work.

I was really happy that only a small group met us at the airport in Christchurch. Fantastic to see them, but just enough people to not be overwhelming. I had considered cycling to the Christchurch flat, but was too tired, and accepted a ride from a good mate while Janie took Ju and all the gear. How nice was it to step into the flat, a familiar place, with food I understood, surplus supplies of things I needed, clothes, cutlery, couches, and I didn't have to hunt for them, a bed I've slept in before, and friends and family to chat to. I'm in my comfort zone, but the journey is not complete. I've still got 140km to cycle to get home, to Hanmer Springs. Time to rebuild Fiona.

Alone, I cycle the streets of Christchurch. For the first time in a very long time, I don't need to use Maps.me to navigate. Instead I meander through the streets, soaking in New Zealand. They drive on the left here. Gotta watch that. I understand all the signage. How great is it to see familiar things again, to smell familiar smells, to understand the culture, the heritage and history? Wow. Yep, even in my own country, there are wows.

My starting point for the cycle home is Bivouac Outdoors. A few people have come to wish me well for this final leg. Fantastic to have them there, and still not overwhelming, which is what I was hoping for. And then my daughter, Lisa, arrives with Ju, and the tears begin. Damn. Graham (the taller one) is joining me on the cycle, and others are shadowing us, making a movie. We haven't gone 5km, and we meet a long-time friend, who just happens to be cycling past. The first of many wonderful hugs, and welcomes. For the next 130km, a car would slow to a stop, and someone would jump out for a photo, a handshake or a hug. They're breaking me in slowly, and it's wonderful.

But now Graham and I are in Kaiapoi, and we're hungry. Oh look, a bakery, Sugar and Spice, and they have pies (oh my, how much have I missed them?) and Belgium Biscuits, and Afghans, and Raspberry buns, and cheese scones, and lolly-cake, and I understand all this, and know what they taste like, and it's like all my dreams coming true.

Ju joins us on the road. She's not yet sick of cycling with me. That's a very good sign. Not long after, Lisa arrives with brother Paul. Tears are flowing again. This emotional stuff is really exhausting. Lisa joins us on a bike, and we are four. And I'm happy, excited, and bouncing. How could it get better? I'm surrounded by family and friends, doing what I really love doing, and heading towards the place I love more than any other in the world.

The plan was to camp, but just as we pulled under the canopy outside the Hurunui Hotel, a vicious thunderstorm struck. Torrential rain and hail, and suddenly a cosy bed in a historic hotel seemed pretty inviting. But the grapevine has been working. Locals are looking out for us. We have several stop in to welcome me home. Every reunion is another special moment, and my sleep is deep.

I'm excited again - only 55km to cycle. Our first stop is the Red Post in Culverden, for an amazingly yummy brunch. We are joined by others on cylces. The peloton now has seven cyclists, more than I've ever cycled with. I'm really happy to share these final kilometres with these friends. 3 miles (5 km) before the Hanmer turnoff, a siren blazes towards us. Bother. An emergency. That's sobering. Nope. It's Fletch and Kaz. How good is it to see them? When skyping from somewhere on my adventure, they always made me cry, and now they've done it again. Buggers.

One more road junction, and I'm home. Oh, my goodness. There's a huge crowd. Fire Engines, Ambulances, and probably forty cyclists, of all ages. Cheering, clapping, yahoos. My vision blurs. Damn it. I want to be able to see the view as I cycle into Hanmer. All I can see is a watery blurred image. Lots of hugs. My face is aching from smiling. As the peloton, which is huge, make our way over the Ferry Bridge, and down the cutting, cyclists come up beside me and welcome me home. There are people waving and cheering along the road, and more cyclists joining the peloton, sirens, and horns. A face from thirty years ago appears and introduces himself. Aaron has driven from Dunedin to welcome me home. I can't believe my adventure has touched so many. It was meant to be my challenge, but somehow it has inspired and moved so many people.

Hanmer is crowded. It's school holidays. People are staring, wondering what the heck is going on, but there's a big crowd at the Heritage Reserve. So many hugs. Oh gosh. My sister and her husband are here, from the Gold Coast. So many faces I've really missed. Oh, it's so great to be home. At the Test of Time gig later that night, I sat in the hall listening. 863 days ago, I had been in this very spot, with the Test of Time playing, at a Going Away Party. It feels as if I've never been away. I'm home, in my happy place.